TRUE CRIME CASE HISTORIES

VOLUME 2

JASON NEAL

AKAMAI PUBLISHING

Cover photos of:

Alyssa Bustamante (upper-left)

Bryan Stewart / Rick Valentini (upper-right)

Robert Napper (bottom-left)

Mark Twitchell (bottom-right)

More books by Jason Neal

Looking for more?? I am constantly adding new volumes of True Crime Case Histories. The series **can be read in any order,** and all books are also available in paperback, hardcover, and audiobook.

Check out the complete series on Amazon

https://amazon.com/author/jason-neal

or

JasonNealBooks.com

**FREE Bonus Book
For My Readers**

**Click to get
your free copy!**

As my way of saying "Thank you" for downloading, I'm giving away a FREE true crime book I think you'll enjoy.

https://TrueCrimeCaseHistories.com

Just click the link above to let me know where to send your free book!

Choose Your Free True Crime Audiobook

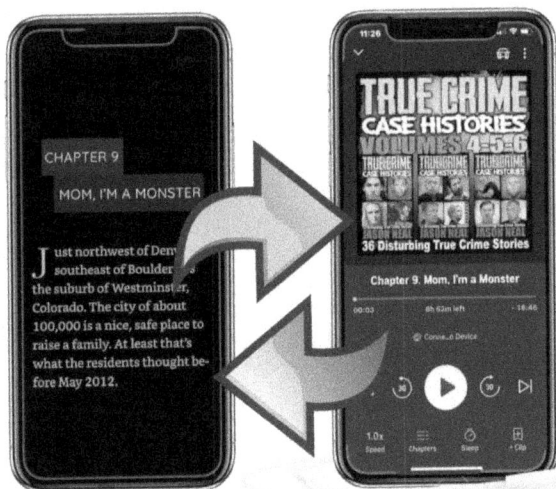

Add Audible Narration and Keep the Story Going!
Plus Get a FREE True Crime Audiobook!

Switch between listening to an audiobook and reading on your Kindle. **Plus choose your first audiobook for FREE!**

https://geni.us/AudibleTrueCrime

CONTENTS

INTRODUCTION

As with Volume One, I'll start with a quick word of warning. The stories you are about to read are brutal and gruesome. They represent humanity at its worst. Television crime shows and stories in the news tend to gloss over the horrible parts, but if you've read the first volume of my series, you know I leave out none of the details. This book is no different. Killing can be a pretty messy endeavor. Consider yourself warned.

When I started this volume of True Crime Case Histories, I didn't have a common theme in mind, just random stories that shocked me. However, as I was writing, I realized a few of them have some similarities.

Two stories deal with killers who stole identities or invented an identity out of thin air. Another two involve killers obsessed with taking photos of their victims – both before and after death. In three stories, police, counselors, and other authorities had plenty of warning signs but ignored them. Similar to Volume One, a few stories involve BDSM (bondage and discipline, domination and submission, sadism and masochism). None of these similarities were intentional, it just happened that way.

––––––––

Trying to understand why killers do what they do can be an exercise in futility. There seems to be no logic other than the fragility of the human mind. Some killers in this book kill out of curiosity. Alyssa Bustamante just wanted to see what taking another person's life was like. Some, like in the case of Myles Fukunaga, killed out of frustration with his own life. Killers who have no control over their anger are probably the most common, like Michael Adams, whose anger was directed toward the one person he loved most. It's a messed up way to show your love if you ask me. Another common trait among killers is mental health issues – murderers like Jamie Reynolds or Robert Napper should have been put away long before they got out of control.

The stories of murder are endless; in this volume, I've added an additional four stories for a total of twelve. I've also added an online appendix for photos, videos, and documents pertaining to the cases. Look for a link to that at the end of the book. I hope you enjoy reading the stories in this volume as much as I've enjoyed researching and writing them.

Lastly, please join my mailing list for discounts, updates, and a free book. You can sign up for that at

TrueCrimeCaseHistories.com

You can also purchase paperbacks, hardcovers, and signed copies of my books directly from me at:

JasonNealBooks.com

Thank you for reading. I sincerely hope you gain some insight from this volume of True Crime Case Histories.

- Jason

CHAPTER 1
THE GIRL IN THE BARREL

On September 2, 1999, in the suburban town of Jericho, New York, just thirty miles from Midtown Manhattan, Ronald Cohen was preparing to sell his house. He had just found a buyer for the property at $455,000, and the new owner wanted to do a final walkthrough before taking ownership.

During the walkthrough, the buyer was very thorough and wanted to see the crawlspace beneath an addition that had been built onto the back of the house about thirty years earlier.

The crawlspace was only thirty-six inches high, so the two men had to hunch down to get through the large space. At the very back of the crawlspace, they noticed a fifty-five-gallon barrel on its side, wedged beneath the stairs. The buyer asked Mr. Cohen about the barrel, but he said it had been there since he bought the property over ten years ago. He had no idea what was in it or how it got there. He had never used the crawlspace, and it was far too heavy to move by himself, so he had just left it there. However, the new buyer said he wanted it removed before purchasing the property. Mr. Cohen and his real estate agent got some help, rolled the barrel out from underneath the home, and took it to the curb for the trash workers to haul away.

When sanitation workers showed up the next day, they informed Mr. Cohen that, at 355 pounds, the barrel was far too heavy for them to take away. They also had no idea what it contained. He would need to empty it to make sure there was nothing hazardous or toxic inside.

Mr. Cohen and his real estate agent decided to open the barrel and separate whatever was inside so it could be disposed of properly. There was a metal seal around the top of the barrel, so they pried it open with some tools. An overwhelming stench immediately hit the two men—the unmistakable stench of death.

Once they had removed the lid, they saw a curled human hand and a woman's shoe. The barrel was filled with a green gooey fluid surrounded by tiny plastic pellets. Mr. Cohen immediately called the police.

———

Investigators took the barrel to the forensics lab, where they emptied it onto a large white tarp so they could collect any evidence. Inside the barrel, they found a small, mummified female body. The body had been crumpled over and bent in half to fit into the barrel. Because the barrel was sealed so tightly, her body had been relatively well preserved, with skin the consistency of rubber. However, the body began decaying quickly after the air hit it, and it was immediately taken away for an autopsy.

During the autopsy, they determined that the body was a female of Hispanic descent. She was tiny, only about four foot nine inches tall, with long black hair and some unusual gold bridgework on her teeth. The bridgework was not commonly done in the United States and had most likely been done somewhere in South America. The cause of death was blunt-force trauma to the head. Someone had used a hammer or similar object to smash her head seven to ten times, crushing her skull. She was also eight to nine months pregnant. Police collected DNA from the fetus to see if they could later match it to a father.

When investigators emptied the rest of the barrel, it oozed out a strange, green, gooey liquid, possibly a chemical dye of some sort. They also noticed tiny black-and-white plastic pellets mixed within the goo. The woman's clothes were still intact and seemed to be a style from the sixties. Near the bottom of the barrel, they found a woman's purse with some cosmetic items inside and a badly damaged address book. There was also a green stem from a plastic flower arrangement.

At the bottom of the barrel were three pieces of jewelry: two gold rings, one with an inscription reading "M.H.R. XII 59," as well as a locket that was engraved, "To Patrice Love Uncle Phil."

The pages of the address book were severely damaged and stuck together with the green goo. Detectives weren't hopeful of getting any clues from it, but just in case, it was put inside a forensic drying cabinet for a few days to dry out.

The following day, detectives began researching where the barrel may have come from. The homeowner, Mr. Cohen, explained that it was already there when he bought the house several years earlier. Detectives began going back through the prior owners to find out who built the extension on the house.

After researching four prior owners, they eventually found the homeowner who had built the extension on the home. He was now seventy-one years old and lived in Boca Raton, Florida. His name was Howard Elkins. He sold the house in 1972 and retired when he closed his plastics business in Manhattan. Police wanted to question him, but they needed to collect more information before making the trip south.

As the days went by, the clues started to pour in. On the side of the barrel were printed the letters "GAF," which turned out to be a chemical company based in New Jersey. Detectives took photos of the barrel and brought some of the pellets and a sample of the green dye to them for analysis. GAF confirmed that they used the polyethylene pellets to make many plastic products, one of those products being plastic flowers. The green dye was a unique product called Halogen Green, specifically used to make plastic flower bases in the 1960s. The only customer they had for that product was Melrose Plastics – the same company that Howard Elkins had closed in 1972.

Meanwhile, the forensic documents lab made some progress on the damaged address book. They got it dried enough to separate the pages, but the ink had utterly disintegrated. Using a video spectral comparator device, they could read some of the information using alternative light sources. The first notation in the book was a number preceded by the letter "A." It was a resident alien number. Detectives spoke with immigration officers, but the number was thirty years old, and their systems had changed since then. It would take time for them to come back with a result.

Knowing that the barrel, the plastic, and the dye all came from Howard Elkins' business, coupled with the fact that they'd found the barrel beneath Elkins' former home, detectives now believed they had enough information to take a trip to Florida and question him. Before questioning him, however, they wanted to visit his former business partner in the plastic flower business – Melvin Gantman, who had also retired to Boca Raton.

Gantman confirmed that he and Elkins were once business partners, but he hadn't spoken to him in years. When shown a photo of the barrel, Gantman quickly confirmed that it was one they often used for their company. He also verified the dye color and plastic pellets were what they used in making their plastic flowers. When shown a photo of the plastic stem found in the barrel, he right away knew it was also from their company.

However, the most helpful information Gantman gave was something he recalled from the late sixties. He knew Elkins had an affair with a Hispanic employee at the company and rented her an apartment. He didn't know her name, but he remembered that she had strange gold teeth in the front and long black hair. Gantman recalled receiving a phone call from the landlord of the apartment Elkins had rented for her. The landlord was looking for Elkins. The apartment was now empty, but the girl's belongings were still in the apartment, and the landlord wanted him to get the things moved out so he could rent it again.

Detectives were now more convinced than ever that seventy-one-year-old Elkins was the killer. They went to his home, and Elkins invited them in. Unfortunately, Elkins couldn't recall all the things that Gantman easily remembered from the business. He had no recollection of the barrel, the dye, or the plastic pellets. Nothing.

Surprisingly, when asked if he'd had an affair during that time, he freely admitted he had. However, all he could say was, "Yes, a very short affair. She left." When asked if he knew she was pregnant or even if he knew her name, he seemed not to remember anything about her.

Detectives informed him that the girl was found pregnant and deceased in a barrel beneath his former house. But Elkins seemed completely unfazed. He flatly refused when they asked him for a sample of his DNA.

Just then, his phone rang. It was his wife. After speaking briefly to his wife, Elkins told the detectives they needed to leave. He said his wife was coming home, and they would have much to discuss.

The New York detectives had no jurisdiction in Florida to get a warrant or make an arrest. Still, before they left, they informed Elkins that they would be back with a warrant and put him in prison for the rest of his life.

———

Early the following morning, the two detectives received a call from the local Palm Beach Police Department. Howard Elkins had disappeared, and his wife had reported him missing.

Friends, family, and the police all searched for Howard Elkins. He was found later that evening in his neighbors' garage in the back seat of their Ford Explorer SUV. That morning, he had gone to Walmart and purchased a 12-gauge Mossberg shotgun. Elkins had sat in the back seat of the

SUV, put the butt of the shotgun between his legs, placed the barrel in his mouth, and shot himself in the head.

There wasn't any question of his guilt, but to be sure, detectives collected his DNA from the scene and took it back to New York, where investigators confirmed he was the father of the unborn baby.

As soon as they returned to New York, eight days after they found the barrel, they got word back from Immigration about the victim's identity. Her name was Reyna Angelica Marroquin, and she had immigrated to the U.S. in 1966 from El Salvador.

The forensic document team also got much more information from the address book. They recovered several names, addresses, and phone numbers. Unfortunately, the phone numbers were over thirty years old; detectives didn't have much hope for them, but they tried calling anyway. Amazingly, one phone number still worked. The woman that answered, Kathy Andrade, was a close friend of Reyna and was still living at the same location three decades later.

Kathy identified Reyna from a thirty-year-old immigration photo. She said Reyna immigrated from El Salvador and worked making plastic flowers at Melrose Plastics in the sixties.

Howard Elkins / Reyna Marroquin

In November 1968, Reyna told Kathy that she had been dating her boss at the flower factory and was pregnant with his baby. Kathy didn't know his name, only that it was Reyna's boss. One day Reyna told her that she had made a terrible mistake. She said she'd gotten mad at him and called his wife. Reyna told Mrs. Elkins that she was having an affair with her husband, he had also promised to marry her, and she was pregnant with his baby. Reyna told Kathy she was terrified that he would kill her. It turns out, her assumption was correct. That was the last time Kathy had ever heard from Reyna.

Kathy recalled going to Reyna's apartment one evening and seeing two plates set out for dinner. Dinner was still warm on the stove, but there was no sign of Reyna. She called the police to report her as missing, but the police told her that she couldn't file a missing person report if she wasn't a family member. She tried to call Reyna every day for weeks after that, but she never heard from her and eventually gave up.

———

Oscar Corral, a journalist covering the story for *Newsday*, a daily newspaper in the New York City area, later tracked down Reyna's ninety-five-year-old mother in San Salvador, El Salvador, and flew down to visit her. Her mother said she would speak to Reyna regularly on the phone, and then suddenly, the calls stopped. She had no idea why. She said she would often dream of Reyna trapped inside a barrel.

Reyna's body was transported back to El Salvador for burial. Her mother died one month later and was buried next to her.

CHAPTER 2

THE MURDER OF JAMIE LAIADDEE

I am always amazed when prosecutors go to trial before a body is found. It's an aggressive move. This is one of those cases. In fact, in this case, there wasn't even physical evidence that a murder had occurred. The prosecutor was Juan Martinez, who became famous years later for prosecuting Jodi Arias, arguably one of the most notorious cases in Arizona history. This case was especially intriguing because it happened near my home in an area I'm extremely familiar with.

———

Jamie Laiaddee grew up in California with her parents, who emigrated from Thailand. Her older sister, Pepper, had graduated from medical school, and Jamie's parents pushed her very hard to do the same. They were obsessively adamant about her getting good grades so she could attend medical school, but Jamie resented the pressure and stress her parents put on her.

When it came time to choose a school, Jamie decided to pursue her degree halfway across the country at the University of Michigan. She created a new life with new friends and excelled in school. Her friends called themselves the "516 Girls," named after the house they shared at 516 Walnut St. in Ann Arbor, Michigan. The girls were diehard fans of their college football team, the University of Michigan Wolverines, and would watch every game together.

After Jamie graduated from college, she got a high-paying job selling medical supplies in Arizona. Her parents pushed and pushed her to go to graduate school, but she was sick of being compared to her sister and cut off contact with her family once she left school.

Arizona was a long way from Michigan, so that meant leaving all her college friends behind and setting out for a new life on her own. She kept in touch with her Michigan friends with phone calls and the occasional wedding, but the girls were now strewn across the world, with some as far away as Germany, Russia, and Australia. In the years after college, it wasn't uncommon to not speak to them for months at a time.

Her new job in Arizona kept her extremely busy with long hours, which also kept her from meeting new people. She decided to join a University of Michigan Alumni group that got together every weekend to watch the Wolverines games at a local bar. It wasn't long before Jamie met a fellow alumnus named Bryan Stewart.

Bryan was good-looking, muscled, charismatic, and just as enthusiastic as Jamie was about Michigan football. He worked as a personal trainer at the local Gold's Gym, and the two hit it off. Within a year, Bryan had moved in with Jamie

to the tract home she'd bought in Chandler, a suburb just
southeast of Phoenix.

Jamie Laiaddee / Bryan Stewart

Jamie, of course, made a lot more money than Bryan, but she
didn't seem to mind. She covered most of the bills, and from
the outside, the two lived a normal life for the next two
years.

The economy was hit hard in the Phoenix area during the
financial crisis of the mid-2000s. As a result, the house Jamie
had purchased earlier was now "upside down," meaning that
she owed more to the bank than the property was worth.
That was fine until August 2009, when Jamie lost her high-
paying job with the medical supplies company. She looked
for a new job for several months, but the prospects weren't
good during those times.

Her money supply was dwindling – and so was Bryan and
Jamie's love affair. Jamie had always been quiet and reserved,
but when the money started draining and the job selection
grew slim, Jamie became despondent; her affection dropped
off.

It didn't help that Bryan had problems with the law. To hear Bryan tell it, he was "wrongfully accused" of trespassing. It was all just a big, silly mistake. But, in reality, he was caught breaking into a Mercedes and was charged with burglary. He missed his court dates several times and was re-arrested a few times. Each time, Jamie would faithfully pay his bail. He had an excuse for her every time. As far as she knew, he didn't have any court dates at all – he only told her that he was "meeting with lawyers."

Bryan decided it was time to end their relationship, so he got his own apartment in nearby Scottsdale. However, he didn't tell Jamie about the apartment until he was ready to move out; on the night of March 17, 2010, he broke the news to her.

But before he had a chance, Jamie had some news of her own. Jamie told Bryan she had been offered a job in Denver, Colorado. She had always told him that she didn't like the Phoenix area, so she was excited to go to Denver and start a new life again. She wanted him to go with her.

However, Bryan didn't like the idea. He wanted nothing to do with Denver and had already decided to break up with her. He told her he thought it was better if she went her way, and he went his. The two argued for a bit, but according to Bryan, they calmed down and went to bed.

Bryan had to be at work early in the morning, so he kissed her goodbye and left at around 3:45 a.m. A few weeks later, Bryan emailed the president of their Michigan Alumni club to tell her that he and Jamie had broken up, and she was moving to Denver to start a new life.

Of course, this whole backstory was just Bryan's distorted truth. It was the story he told Jamie's friends and, later, the police. The actual truth was very different.

———

Jamie didn't have any close friends other than Bryan in the Phoenix area. The others at the alumni club were more acquaintances than friends. She wasn't on the greatest terms with her parents and hadn't spoken to them in quite a while. Her best friends were her friends from college, but she hadn't kept in regular contact with them either. Thus, it was no wonder nobody noticed when there had been no contact from Jamie for almost three months.

Bryan still attended the alumni meetings, but her friends were getting anxious. They had sent her numerous emails, but she wasn't responding. Even if she had moved to Denver, she would have had the courtesy to return their emails. Finally, the alumni friends pressured Bryan to call her parents. He finally reached her estranged father in California and told him that his daughter was missing.

Jamie's father immediately called the Chandler police, and they stopped by Jamie's home to do a welfare check. Officers looked in the garage windows and saw that her 1999 Honda was parked there, but her 2007 Ford Explorer was missing. When detectives spoke to a neighbor, he told them that there used to be a man and woman living there, but he hadn't seen them in a long time.

The neighbor also mentioned that someone from a local Phoenix company showed up a few days prior and said they had hired Jamie for a job. The man said he gave her a laptop, cell phone, and credit card, but she never showed up for her first day at work. Assuming she had decided not to take the job, the man was there to collect the items.

Police broke into Jamie's house to find it extremely messy, but there was no sign of a struggle, and it didn't seem that anyone had tried to clean up a crime scene. It was just an unkept, cluttered house with mail on the table and clothes thrown about.

Inside the house, they found her passport, clothes, and suitcases, but her driver's license and purse were missing, so it was plausible she'd left somewhere on her own accord.

Knowing that Jamie owned a second vehicle, police put out an alert to watch for it. Many police cars in the Phoenix area had license plate readers – in addition to police cars, they were on traffic cameras, entry gates, toll booths, and many other places. These were scanning devices that continually scanned license plates and stored the data in a massive database. Police were able to track the whereabouts of almost any vehicle very quickly.

The databases tracked Jamie's Ford Escape just eighteen miles away in Scottsdale. The plates were regularly seen entering the gate of a condo complex. Chandler detectives staked out the condo and waited for the SUV to arrive. When it did, Bryan Stewart was driving.

When detectives asked Bryan why he was driving his girlfriend's car, he immediately corrected them, "Ex-girlfriend." He told them he had a perfectly good excuse for driving her car. He claimed she had given it to him as a parting gift before she left for her new life in Denver. But, of course, detectives didn't believe his story.

Bryan had been driving on an expired driver's license, so they arrested him and got a warrant to search his condo.

Bryan asked if he could go to the bathroom before they drove back down to Chandler, but the police denied his request. They suspected he wanted to hide something in his condo before they searched it. When they made the thirty-minute drive back to Chandler, he strangely didn't need to use the restroom anymore.

Bryan kept a meticulous home, quite the opposite of Jamie. As investigators searched his condo, they noticed everything was in perfect order to the point of being indicative of OCD. However, one thing seemed out of place: a woman's wallet was sitting on his desk. Inside the wallet were several of Jamie's credit cards. When investigators searched the purchase records they found that Bryan had been using the cards to purchase camping supplies online, shopping at Target, Costco, and Walmart, and even buying subscriptions to online dating websites.

One of the cards was an American Express business card. The company name was CareFusion. Police later discovered that this was the company that had hired Jamie in Phoenix, not Denver. They had issued her a laptop, cell phone, and credit card.

But even more interesting was a copy of his birth certificate that they found. It was handwritten, whereas most birth certificates are typed. It seemed very suspicious.

They also found an envelope addressed to someone named Rick Wayne Valentini at a different address in Scottsdale. They thought Bryan may have been stealing someone's mail, but they knew something was wrong when they found a divorce decree in his filing cabinet for Rick Wayne Valentini from Michigan.

Police called the wife listed on the divorce decree and quickly realized that Bryan Stewart and Rick Valentini were the same person. The ex-wife explained to police that she'd divorced Rick Valentini several years ago when he had stolen money from her father and fled to Arizona. Rick Valentini told her he planned to change his name so he wouldn't have to pay child support.

She also mentioned to police that Rick was once physically and verbally abusive to her. Police now had enough to bring fraud charges on Bryan and keep him in jail for long enough to investigate whether he had something to do with the disappearance of Jamie Laiaddee.

When detectives confronted him and told him they knew he was Rick Valentini, he freely admitted it. He said he wasn't running from the law but was desperately trying to leave behind a troubled life. He claimed to have had a very traumatic childhood. His mother was only eighteen when she gave birth to him, and his father didn't want anything to do with him. He said his mother forced him to live in the garage for years until she finally sent him to foster care. He said the only love and attention he got as a child was from his aunts and uncles. Police contacted his aunt, who verified his story that he was physically and emotionally abused during his childhood, but detectives didn't have much sympathy for him.

As investigators looked further into Rick Valentini's past, they realized that he actually had three ex-wives. He also had two daughters he never visited nor paid child support for. In addition, the ex-wives all painted him as a pathological liar.

They also found that he was eight years older than he let on. His actual Rick Valentini birth certificate didn't match his Bryan Stewart Arizona driver's license.

The lies just kept piling up. Bryan claimed he'd spent time in the military in Iraq and Afghanistan. He was indeed in the military, but the truth was he'd never been to either of those places. He went AWOL (Absent Without Leave), and when military police arrested him, he stabbed an officer in the hand and leg. He then spent two years in a military prison.

And then there was his University of Michigan story. As expected, despite the diploma for the University of Michigan hanging on his wall and his University of Michigan ID card, Bryan had never attended college. He had forged the diploma and ID, just like he had done with the Bryan Stewart birth certificate. The University of Michigan didn't even offer an "Education Physiology" degree like his diploma stated.

Bryan then revealed that he had an explanation for Jamie's disappearance. He told detectives that Jamie had lost her job and she was about to lose her house. She hated her parents and hated Arizona and wanted to disappear so that she could create another life – a completely new identity. Who better to help her than someone who had experience creating a new identity? He said she wanted him to go with her, but he refused. Instead, he agreed to help her disappear.

He also claimed he had been in contact with her a few times since she left and that she had even been to his Scottsdale condo. He said he had given her a key to his condo, and he sometimes noticed that she had been there while he was gone, claiming she had moved things around inside the condo.

Police still didn't believe his lies but needed more evidence to charge him with anything other than fraud. They wanted to charge him with murder, but there was still no evidence that anything had happened to Jamie.

Further searches of Bryan's condo revealed Jamie's cell phone and a small white envelope in the back of a filing cabinet. Jamie's Arizona driver's license was inside the envelope, cut up into about 30 pieces. Bryan claimed that Jamie cut the license up herself, but the DNA on the flap of the envelope proved that Bryan had licked the envelope and sealed it, not Jamie.

Going through Bryan's bank statements, they noticed a charge to a self-storage facility. Police thought this was their lucky break. Maybe he'd hidden the body or other evidence of a crime. Investigators didn't find a smoking gun, but they did find several weapons, such as hatchets, swords, a sawed-off shotgun, a semi-automatic handgun, a shovel with clumped dirt on it, and a roll of thick, black plastic liner.

In Arizona, there are endless miles of desert. He could have easily used the shovel to dig a grave and the thick plastic liner to wrap her body. But, again, there was no blood evidence or anything that prosecutors could use to get a conviction.

Next were Jamie's credit card statements. They saw Jamie had paid to run an online background check just before her disappearance. Detectives believed she had found out about Bryan's lies. She may have discovered that he had ex-wives, children, never went to the University of Michigan, and that Bryan wasn't even his real name. But still, nothing was solid enough that they were willing to risk going to trial.

Fortunately, the break they needed was coming. While in jail, one of Bryan's cellmates told his defense attorney that he had some information he was willing to share to get his sentence reduced. The informant said that Bryan talked to him about hiding a body.

"He told me, 'I wish I knew where they were looking.'... he's wondering where you guys are looking for the body. If you guys are getting warm."

The informant also claimed that Bryan told him he shot her with a sawed-off shotgun and got rid of the body where "nobody will ever find it." Then, he said Bryan questioned, "What can they charge me with if they can't find a body?"

It wasn't much, but the jailhouse confession was enough to convince prosecutors to charge him with second-degree murder. The prosecutor assigned was Juan Martinez.

————

The Bryan Stewart / Rick Valentini trial began in October 2011. The first witness was a personal training client of Bryan's. She testified that Bryan constantly complained about his relationship with Jamie, saying she was his "sugar mama" and calling her a "whining, nagging bitch."

The next witness was from CareFusion, the employer who had offered Jamie a job – not in Denver, as Bryan had claimed, but nearby in Phoenix. Another witness was a friend of Jamie's who testified that he'd seen her covered with bruises just d

Jamie Laiddee / Bryan Stewart aka Rick Valentini

ays before she went missing.

The thing that put the nail in Valentini's coffin, though, was when he took the stand in his own defense, despite his lawyer's warnings. On the stand, he told the same old stories he had told the police. It didn't work, and the jury didn't buy it. With only four hours of deliberation, the jury returned with a guilty verdict even without a body or physical evidence that a murder had occurred.

Rick Valentini was sentenced to a total of fifty-four years in prison: twenty-two years for second-degree murder, twenty years for fraud, and twelve more years for other crimes related to the murder.

Eight years after her death, the remains of Jaime Laiaddee were found in a work lot that held large piles of decorative rock for a landscaping supply company. Medical examiners stated her bones were too degraded to determine a cause of death.

CHAPTER 3
THE DEXTER WANNABE

"Drive down the alley and park in the gravel driveway next to the garage. I'll leave the garage door partly open, so you can sneak in underneath. Then close the garage door behind you."

Those aren't exactly the typical instructions you would expect from a girl you're meeting for a first date, but that's similar to what Gilles Tetreault received. Gilles had been chatting on the dating site plentyoffish.com with a girl named Sheena, and it was to be their first meeting.

But Sheena didn't exist. Gilles followed the strange instructions and snuck in underneath the garage door to find himself in a dark garage with a man in a hockey mask and a blue light sparkling in his hand. The blue light was from an 800-volt stun baton the man shoved at Gilles' stomach. He immediately fell to the ground and convulsed as his attacker stuck duct tape over his eyes.

Gilles managed to tear the duct tape off his eyes only to find a handgun pointed straight at his face. He could tell from the eyes peering through the hockey mask that this crazy person intended to end his life. That's when he made the split-second decision to try to grab the gun from his attacker – but the moment he got his hands on the weapon, he had a revelation. The gun was made of plastic. It was a fake. Gilles released his grip from the gun, fell to the floor, and rolled as fast as he could back under the garage door and into the alley.

Once outside the garage, Gilles realized that he couldn't run. The shock from the stun baton had made his legs temporarily useless. He tried to crawl down the gravel alley while his attacker pulled him by the legs back toward the garage. Gilles looked up and saw a man and woman walking their dog and watching the whole ordeal. He called to them for help, but his attacker laughed and said, "Come on, Frank, let's go back in the garage." The attacker was trying to make the couple believe it was all a silly game.

The couple walked away, worried that it was a trick and the two men were trying to rob them. The attacker hid back in the garage, which allowed Gilles the chance to crawl his way into his truck and drive away.

Afraid and embarrassed, Gilles didn't report the attack to the police. Not reporting the crime, however, was a grave mistake. The whole episode would be repeated a week later with a different victim.

———

Johnny Altinger was a tall, thirty-eight-year-old tech worker looking for love on plentyoffish.com. Johnny had a close group of friends he kept in touch with daily, and he told them he had been chatting with a girl named Jen. He was planning on meeting her that evening.

Johnny had shared his conversations with Jen with several friends until he pulled into the alleyway at 7 p.m. on October 10, 2008. Unfortunately, that was the last time anyone heard from him.

It was a holiday weekend in Canada, and his friends were getting worried when Johnny didn't show up for a motor-cycle trip they had planned together.

The following Monday, several of his friends received similar emails from Johnny's email address:

> "Hey there, I've met an extraordinary woman named Jen who has offered to take me on a nice long tropical vacation. We'll be staying in her winter home in Costa Rica. Phone number to follow soon. I won't be back in town until December 10, but I will be checking my email periodically.
>
> See you around the holidays,
>
> -Johnny"

This was clearly out of character for Johnny, and his friends didn't believe he had written the email. Their worry escalated when they called his workplace to find that he hadn't shown up. Concern turned to frustration when they called the police, who refused to do anything.

Johnny's friends took matters into their own hands and broke into his apartment. Once inside, they found his clothes, suitcase, and passport. There was no way he could have gone on a tropical vacation without his passport. With this new information, they went back to the police.

Detective Bill Clark handled the case. He usually dealt with homicide rather than missing person cases, but he knew something was wrong in this instance. Luckily, Johnny's friends had a critical piece of information: they knew the exact directions to the house where the date with Jen was supposed to have taken place.

Police contacted the person renting the home and brought him in for an interview. His name was Mark Twitchell.

Twitchell was an aspiring independent filmmaker. He had produced a low-budget Star Wars fan film and was working on another film inspired by his favorite TV show, Dexter.

During the interview, Twitchell seemed genuinely surprised that someone may have used his garage for an assault. He gladly offered to show them around the garage, which he used as his makeshift movie studio.

When he showed them around, he told the police that the padlock on the garage door wasn't his. It seemed that someone had switched the lock on the door. Once inside, he showed detectives the props he used for his films and even showed the script he was working on called "House of Cards."

The House of Cards storyline featured a serial killer who found his victims on the Internet and lured them back to his "kill room," where he would use a stun baton and a hockey mask to incapacitate his victims.

Police had their suspicions about Twitchell, but without a body or evidence of a murder, they had no reason to hold him. They had to let him go. Afterward, Detective Clark re-watched the video of the initial interview with Twitchell and believed he was being honest and upfront: just a movie geek making low-budget films. They had no idea that Twitchell's movie script matched perfectly with what had happened to Johnny Altinger.

Just after the interview and in a bizarre move, Twitchell sent an email to detectives titled "More info that might be useful." In this email, he claimed that he suddenly remembered that he had bought a car from a man at a gas station. He explained that a random man approached him and said he wanted to sell his car. Twitchell only had $40 on him at the time, and the man accepted it. The car was a red Mazda worth about $20,000. Twitchell claimed the man said he had met a rich "sugar mama" who would buy him a new car when they returned from vacation.

The story was all too bizarre for Detective Clark to believe. He looked up the car Twitchell claimed to have purchased for $40 and discovered it was a red Mazda registered to Johnny Altinger. This information tied Twitchell directly to Johnny and made him their primary – and only – suspect. However, they still had no reason to hold him or even issue a search warrant without evidence that a crime had been committed.

Detective Clark decided to go to the public for help. That was when the couple that had been walking their dog down the alley came forward. When they heard the news, they assumed they had watched the attack of John Altinger and told their story to the police. But police quickly realized that the attack the couple described had happened a week earlier than Johnny's disappearance. Police now realized there may be a second victim out there, with no idea if the person was alive or dead.

———

A month after his attack, Gilles Tetreault heard the news that Johnny had gone missing from the same garage where he was attacked. He knew it must have been the same attacker. The discovery compelled him to go to the police and finally tell his story.

The news of Gilles Tetreault's attack confirmed detectives' suspicion that a crime had been committed in the garage; they believed Twitchell was responsible. A search warrant was issued for Twitchell's car and the house he was renting. When investigators arrived, they found mountains of evidence.

Upon searching the garage, investigators found the hockey mask, stun baton, garbage bags, duct tape, knives, plastic coveralls, and a pellet pistol, all with traces of blood. Blood was all over the walls, floor, and "kill table." There was even an empty water pitcher with blood residue all over it. Twitchell had claimed that the blood was fake and the other items were movie props, but further testing showed the blood was real. It was human blood and the DNA matched Johnny Altinger.

The trunk of Twitchell's car had a massive pool of dried blood, and in the back seat, they found his laptop covered with Spiderman stickers.

Mark Twitchell

When computer forensic experts got inside the laptop, they found the most damning evidence of all. In the deleted files, they found a file titled "SK Confessions." The text was horrifying. It was a detailed account of his butchering and dismemberment of Johnny Altinger. It even spoke of the previous victim that narrowly escaped.

(A full copy of the "SK Confessions" document and evidence photos are available in the appendix at the end of this book.)

Detectives arrested Mark Twitchell on Halloween. They held him in jail for months while detectives poured through the evidence and built a case against him. They still needed a body to help their case and to offer closure to Johnny's friends and family. Months and months went by, but Twitchell refused to say a word about what he had done with the body.

The text of "SK Confessions" went into graphic detail about how he had dismembered the body and put it down a storm drain. It said nothing, however, about where that storm drain was. Police searched sewers within a one-mile radius of

Twitchell's home using snaking cameras but had no luck discovering the remains.

Twitchell still wouldn't speak, so detective Green put him in the back of his police car and drove him around for hours near the murder scene, trying to get him to disclose the location. But his plan didn't work.

Twitchell got a new lawyer several months later, and detectives received a phone call. He finally wanted to tell them where the body was, possibly thinking his cooperation would help his case or reduce his sentence. His lawyer gave police a map printed out from Google maps with exact directions to the storm drain where he claimed to have dumped Johnny Altinger's body. It was only a few blocks from Twitchell's home.

During the trial, Mark Twitchell took the stand in his own defense. His lawyers tried to paint him as a regular guy. Just a young man with Hollywood ambitions. They claimed he planned to lure a few men to the garage, scare them, and let them go, hoping they would tell their story and it would be good publicity for his upcoming movie.

The story was ludicrous, and the jury didn't believe it. After only four hours of deliberation, the jury returned a guilty verdict. On April 12, 2011, Mark Twitchell was sentenced to life in prison with no parole for a minimum of twenty-five years.

CHAPTER 4
THE MURDER OF ELIZABETH OLTEN

It was an ordinary Wednesday evening. Nine-year-old Elizabeth Olten was home with her mother when there was a knock on the door. It was their six-year-old neighbor, Emma. Emma wanted to see if Elizabeth could come out and play at her house.

Elizabeth's mother initially denied their request because she was making dinner and it would be ready soon, but the girls were persistent, and she allowed Elizabeth to go out for just an hour. Dinner was at 6 p.m., so she told her to be home by then. No later.

When Elizabeth didn't come home at 6 p.m., her mother immediately called her cell phone. There was no answer. When her mother called Emma's house, Emma said Elizabeth had started walking home several minutes ago. But they only lived four houses away – she should have had plenty of time for to make it home by 6 p.m. Elizabeth's mother was panic-stricken. She knew Elizabeth was afraid of the dark and would never walk home alone after dark. She immediately called the police.

Word spread quickly of Elizabeth's disappearance, and within a few hours, hundreds of people were involved in the search. The tiny town of St. Martin, Missouri, had only a little over 1,000 people, but more than 300 residents helped in the search. Police jumped into action too. They had planes, helicopters, dogs, and even emergency divers to search nearby ponds and rivers.

Theories started to spread. Had a child molester abducted her? Had someone kidnapped her? Police set up checkpoints on all roads leaving town and checked in with any registered sex offenders in the area, but there were no clues at all.

By the next day, the FBI was involved, and an extensive investigation began. Using information from Elizabeth's cell phone, they triangulated an approximate position: her cell phone was in the thick, wooded area directly behind their homes. But they had already searched that area and turned up nothing.

In the wooded area, local volunteers found a hole in the ground. It seemed to be a makeshift grave. The FBI processed the hole and the surrounding area, but still, they found nothing to help the investigation.

FBI agents began by looking at the last person who saw Elizabeth, which was six-year-old Emma. This time Emma added to her story. She claimed she was playing outside with Elizabeth, but Emma got stuck in some thorn bushes and ran crying for her older stepsister, Alyssa. She said she left Elizabeth there by herself near the bushes.

The older stepsister, fifteen-year-old Alyssa Bustamante, had skipped school that day. That was different for Alyssa; she was an A and B student who rarely missed school. Alyssa was a normal kid whose friends said she was fun to be around. She attended church at the Church of Jesus Christ of Latter-day Saints and regularly joined in with the youth programs there.

When FBI agents questioned Alyssa, she denied knowing anything about Elizabeth's whereabouts. She explained that she had indeed skipped school that day, but that had nothing to do with the missing girl. She seemed very calm and collected. A normal teenage kid – certainly nothing to raise suspicions with the FBI agents.

Alyssa Bustamante

During the interview, Alyssa admitted she had dug the hole. "I just like digging holes," she said. Alyssa claimed she would occasionally bury dead animals that she found in the woods behind her home.

While they questioned her, other FBI agents searched the house using their search warrants. Everything throughout the house seemed to be in place, but when they entered Alyssa's room, they found there was a much darker side to the young girl.

The walls of Alyssa's bedroom were covered with writings and drawings. One crude drawing was an outline of a human figure which seemed to have slash marks across its arms. Next to the image was the word "Emma," referring to

Alyssa's younger stepsister. Some of the writings on the walls seemed to form poems:

"I cut to focus.

I cut when my brain is racing.

I cut to make physical what I feel inside.

I cut to see blood because I like it.

I don't like to cut, but I can't give it up."

Another said:

"It was written in blood.

IT WAS WRITTEN IN BLOOD!"

Also taped to the walls were cards, photos, and letters from her father, who was currently in prison. In fact, both of Alyssa's parents were incarcerated. Alyssa had a difficult upbringing; when she was six, her mother, Michelle Bustamante, had a drug overdose right in front of her. Her mother had several drug and alcohol convictions, while her father, Caesar Bustamante, was in prison for assault. By 1998, her grandmother, Karen Brooke, gained custody of her and brought Alyssa to the tiny town to give her a somewhat normal life. However, Alyssa had problems – dark psychological problems. She was good at hiding them from the general public, but to her close friends and family, could change from a good girl to a completely different personality. On her fifteenth birthday, a friend recalled Alyssa asking,

"Have you ever wondered what it would be like to kill someone?"

Her darker persona especially came out online. She posted photos of herself with mascara and lipstick smeared all over her face, with her fingers pointed like a gun to her head. A post on her Twitter feed read: "Bad decisions make great stories." On YouTube and MySpace, she listed her hobbies as "killing people" and "cutting." One of her videos uploaded to YouTube showed her coaching her younger twin brothers to touch an electric fence.

On Labor Day, when Alyssa was thirteen, she tried to kill herself by taking a handful of pills. Her grandmother found her on the bathroom floor. She spent ten days in a psychiatric hospital, bounced from therapist to therapist, and was prescribed anti-depressants.

Finally, just a few weeks before Elizabeth went missing, a panel of psychiatrists determined that Alyssa should be committed, long-term, to a hospital. She was then diagnosed with an antisocial personality disorder. However, instead of hospitalizing her, they decided to double her prescription.

———

When the FBI agents searched Alyssa's room, they found her diary. The diary had some extremely disturbing entries, with many about self-harm and "cutting." Alyssa was known to be a cutter – a person who physically cuts their own body and inflicts pain upon themselves through self-mutilation. It's believed that many cutters use physical pain to temporarily relieve the pain of depression or anxiety. Alyssa had over 300 cut wounds, burn marks, and bite marks all over her body, all self-inflicted.

Other entries in the diary included talk of burning down a house with the people inside it. Another entry from October 14, one week before Elizabeth went missing, said,

> "If I don't talk about it, I bottle it up, and when I explode, someone's gonna die."

However, the entry that FBI agents were most interested in was from October 21, the day Elizabeth went missing. That day had an entry scribbled through heavily in blue ink; she obviously didn't want anyone to see what she had written. Only one part of the entry was still visible. At the very end, it read,

> "…I gotta go to church now…lol".

Using a bit of simple backlighting, agents made out two additional words: "slit" and "throat." They then knew there was a lot more to this story.

Agents brought Alyssa into the FBI headquarters for more questioning. Meanwhile, the forensics lab went to work on the scribbled-out section of her diary.

As she was only fifteen, Alyssa was accompanied by her grandmother, who was her legal guardian at the time.

Detectives toyed with Alyssa during her interrogation. They knew she was involved but didn't know exactly to what extent. During the interrogation, they built on her stress levels with long periods of silence strictly to make her uncomfortable. It's a tactic that police use to draw out stress in suspects. The tactic worked, and Alyssa started to physically shake.

Detectives told her they had read her diary, even the last entry that she had scribbled out. They actually hadn't, but they wanted her to believe they had. Finally, Alyssa broke down and told the detectives it was an accident. She claimed they were walking in the woods when Elizabeth fell and hit her head on a rock. She said she tried to revive her, but Elizabeth had died.

The police didn't believe her, and they let her know it. They told Alyssa they would recover the body, and it would show the truth. They told her that a throat doesn't get slit by hitting your head on a rock. Detectives then asked her point blank, "Was her throat cut?" and Alyssa replied, "Yes."

Her grandmother couldn't take anymore. She started crying and left the interrogation room. Seeing her grandmother so disgusted with her broke Alyssa, and she told the entire story to the FBI agents.

Alyssa admitted that she sent her little sister, Emma, to Elizabeth's house specifically to get her and then sent Emma back home. She then took Elizabeth's hand and led her into the woods. "I have a surprise for you," she told the little girl. They walked deep into the woods and reached a hole in the ground. It was a grave that Alyssa had dug five days earlier.

Alyssa confessed that she strangled the nine-year-old, stabbed her in the chest seven times, and then slit her throat with a kitchen knife. One thrust to the chest was forceful enough to pierce the chest bone, cut through the top of the heart, and lodge the tip of the knife into her spine. She then rolled the body into the grave. Alyssa covered Elizabeth lightly with dirt and branches and walked home as if nothing had happened. She put the kitchen knife into the dishwasher and went to her bedroom to clean up.

The forensic lab used a blue light device to recover the full text of Alyssa's diary entry from the day of the murder. It showed that Alyssa took pleasure in killing the poor girl.

> "I just fucking killed someone. I strangled them and slit their throat and stabbed them. Now they're dead. I don't know how to feel atm [at the moment]."

> "It was ahmazing. As soon as you get over the 'ohmygawd I can't do this' feeling, it's pretty enjoyable. I'm kinda nervous and shaky though right now. Kay, I gotta go to church now... lol."

It was clear that the murder of Elizabeth Olten was premeditated. Alyssa had dug two graves five days before the murder and had sent her little sister to Elizabeth's house to get her. She had also spent at least fifteen minutes walking with the little girl – time to consider her actions.

Alyssa led police to the grave she had dug, and they found the body of Elizabeth buried inside, just as she had explained. It was in the same area where they had gotten the cell phone pings and had been searching the entire time.

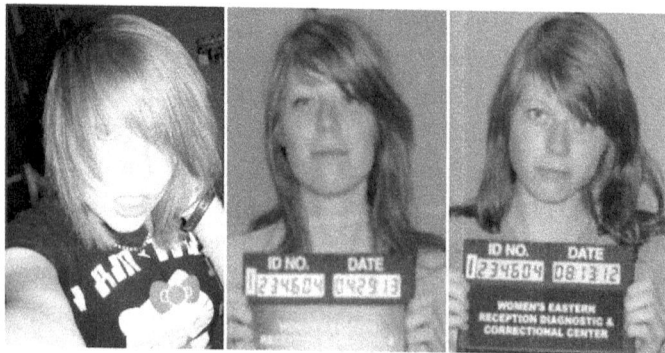

Alyssa Bustamante

In Missouri, despite being only fifteen years old at the time, Alyssa's crimes met the requirements for her to be tried as an adult and charged with first-degree murder. That made her eligible for the death penalty. She was charged with two counts of first-degree murder and one count of armed criminal action.

However, in a setback to the prosecution, some tactics used during her interrogation were not allowed on a juvenile in Missouri. The judge then threw out Alyssa's confession.

Additionally, the US Supreme Court was about to pass a law that life sentences without the possibility of parole for juveniles were to be deemed unconstitutional.

Prosecutors then offered the defense a plea deal. If she accepted a charge of second-degree murder, she would serve a life sentence with a chance of parole in ten to thirty years. They took the deal, but Elizabeth's family was livid with the outcome.

During her sentencing, Alyssa addressed Elizabeth's family directly:

> "I know words can never be enough, and they can never adequately describe how horribly I feel for all of this. If I could give my life to get her back, I would. I'm sorry."

But the words were too little, too late; the family believed she was only saying that after being coached by her defense team in hopes of getting a lighter sentence.

The prosecution argued for life in prison plus seventy-one years – the years that Elizabeth could have lived. Prosecutor Mark Richardson said, "These sentences are appropriate to fit what happened to Elizabeth at the hands of a truly evil individual who strangled and stabbed an innocent child simply for the thrill of it."

The defense argued that Alyssa's depression and suicide attempts should allow her a reduced sentence, but the prosecution reminded the judge that Alyssa's actions were cold and deliberate. She knew exactly what she was doing and had time to think about it before doing it.

Alyssa was ultimately sentenced to life in prison plus thirty years for armed criminal action. Under Missouri law, Alyssa will serve thirty-five years and five months before she's eligible for parole in 2044.

A year after the conviction, Elizabeth's mother, Patricia Preiss, sued Alyssa for a wrongful death suit and settled the lawsuit for $5 million, but it's doubtful she'll ever see a cent of that money.

She also attempted to sue Pathways Behavior Healthcare and two of its employees, as Alyssa was under their care when she murdered Elizabeth. Patricia believed they knew of Alyssa's tendencies and could have prevented the death by institutionalizing her. However, the judge threw out the lawsuit.

CHAPTER 5

INTERPOL'S MOST WANTED

On July 28, 1996, off the coast of Southwest England, a fishing trawler was having trouble getting their full catch for the day. So the captain decided to sail a little further out to sea, to an area where they rarely ventured. Fishing there for a while, they thought they had struck a big haul when they pulled up the net; the net was much heavier than usual. They initially thought possibly a dolphin had become stuck in the net, but when they pulled it up, they realized they had snagged a human body.

Once on board, they saw it was the body of a fully clothed man. He was wearing a Rolex watch, had a maple leaf tattoo on the back of his hand, and his pants pockets had been turned inside out. He was severely bruised and had a massive gash on the top of his head. The fishermen radioed the police, told them what they had found, and headed back into the harbor.

Devon and Cornwall Police brought the body in for an autopsy. Though his head had a massive wound, his lungs were filled with water. He was alive while in the water and had drowned. The gash on the head could have come from something he hit while in the water. The English Channel area had vast amounts of coastline, and drownings were not uncommon. Investigators assumed the man could have died during a boating accident or even by suicide.

The Rolex Oyster Perpetual watch on his wrist was water-proof and self-winding. Police contacted Rolex and found that Rolex self-winding watches kept the correct time for about forty hours without wrist movement; the watch had stopped at 11:35 a.m. on the 22nd. From the amount of decomposition, they knew the body hadn't been in the water for over a month, so they determined that the watch had stopped on July 22. That made the approximate time of death sometime on July 20.

Rolex also informed them that all Rolex watches had a serial number etched just beneath where the band meets the body of the watch. From the serial number, they could find the owner of the watch from purchase and servicing records. Using the serial number, detectives discovered the Rolex belonged to a man named Ronald Platt, whose address was listed in Chelmsford, Essex, 250 miles east of where the body was found.

In an attempt to contact the next of kin, police first contacted the rental agent of Ronald Platt's flat. The agent only had one contact, which was the reference he listed when renting the flat. The reference was a man named David Davis.

When police contacted Davis, he seemed genuinely sad to hear of Ron's passing. Davis spoke with an American accent and was very personable. He let the detectives know that he was a good friend of Ronald. Ronald had dated a woman that had worked for Davis – they had moved to Canada together but had recently moved back separately. Davis said the last time he talked to Ronald was about six weeks ago when he mentioned he was starting a new business in France.

Dental records confirmed that the body was indeed that of Ronald Platt and detectives now assumed the death was an accident. He had probably fallen off a boat on the way to France.

However, police still needed a signature from a friend or family to add to the coroner's report, so they decided to travel to Devon to the home of David Davis.

The country roads near Davis' home in Devon didn't have house numbers, so when police arrived, they knocked on the first door along the road. The man who answered the door explained they were at the wrong address. The address they were looking for was the next house down the road, but the man was curious and asked why they were looking for his neighbor. The detectives explained they were looking for David Davis, and the man had a perplexed look on his face.

> "There's no David Davis living there. That's the home of Ronald Platt."

The detectives were confused and continued asking the man more questions. The man insisted his neighbor was named Ronald Platt and lived there with his much younger wife, Noel Platt.

Something was obviously wrong here and detectives were very suspicious. They then decided against knocking on David Davis' door and went back to the police station to do some digging.

Davis had mentioned to them that Ronald Platt had been dating a woman named Elaine Boyce. Investigators located Elaine and informed her that Ronald Platt was dead. She explained that she had been in a relationship with Ronald for thirteen years but they had split up two years ago when they returned from Canada. When she heard the news, she immediately assumed Ronald had committed suicide. Ron had always been a very passive, shy, and quiet man.

However, when the police mentioned David Davis, she knew something was terribly wrong. Police told her they had spoken to Davis four weeks ago and told him of Ron's death. However, Elaine had spoken to Davis just two weeks ago, and he had mentioned nothing of it. She knew Davis was hiding something. Elaine also said that she knew Ron had been in the Devon area in the days leading up to his death.

Police decided to look through Davis' phone and financial records around July 20, the time of Ron Platt's death. They found that David Davis owned a yacht in South Devon called The Lady Jane. This information wasn't enough for a conviction of anything, being that they had no proof that Ron's death wasn't an accident, but they decided to risk it and arrest him anyway.

With only suspicion of murder, police arrested David Davis on October 31, 1997. They found fifty-one-year-old Davis there with his twenty-one-year-old wife and two babies. During the arrest, his young wife was packing a diaper bag for the babies, but police noticed the bag seemed extremely heavy.

When officers looked through the diaper bag, they found £4,000 in British currency and two large 1 kg gold bars. During the house raid, they found more currency; British pounds, Swiss francs, French francs, more gold bars, and expensive fine art paintings worth around $290,000.

Detectives were now at a turning point. They still had no evidence of a murder, but it was obvious Davis had stolen Ronald Platt's identity. They just didn't know why. The Crown Prosecution Service gave the detectives a week to come up with some definitive evidence or they would have to release him.

The detectives started by returning to the crime scene to speak to the fishing boat captain. When they questioned the captain, he pointed out a few details the police had missed. Ron Platt's pants pockets had been turned inside-out, so it was apparent someone had gone through his pockets. If someone accidentally drowns, their pants pockets don't automatically turn out. Also, when they hauled up the body in the fishing net, there was a ten-pound anchor in the same haul. When police asked why he hadn't mentioned that initially, the captain simply replied, "You didn't ask." Police then took the ten-pound anchor into evidence.

When investigators raided Davis' house, they found purchase receipts made with credit cards under Ronald Platt's name. One of those receipts was from a nautical shop in Dartmouth, and among the items on that receipt was a ten-pound anchor. They confirmed the anchor Davis had purchased was the same one hauled up by the fishing boat.

When they found Davis' yacht, forensic investigators went over the boat with a fine-tooth comb. In the boat's hull, they found a shopping bag from the same nautical store where they found the receipt for the anchor. Inside the bag, they found all the other items on the receipt – everything but the anchor. Ron Platt's fingerprints were on that bag, proving he was on the boat.

On a seat cushion in the cabin, they found three hairs attached to a chunk of skin. DNA tests proved the hairs were Ron Platt's. Police assumed they were ripped from Ron's head when Davis hit him over the head with the anchor.

The forensic lab also noticed zinc residue inside Ron Platt's leather belt. That zinc proved similar to the zinc on the anchor. Police believe that Davis had tucked the anchor into Platt's belt, like a sword, before he threw him over the edge.

The boat featured new technology at the time, GPS. The global positioning system proved that the boat was in the same general area where the body was pulled up on July 20, the same day that the Rolex confirmed Ronald Platt had died.

The police now believed they had the evidence they needed to secure a murder conviction. However, the one thing they didn't have was a motive. They still didn't know why David Davis had been posing as Ronald Platt in the first place.

It wasn't until they ran Davis' fingerprints through global databases that they realized exactly who they had captured. The man they had arrested was not David Davis; that was also an assumed name. His real name was Albert Johnson Walker. He was number four on Interpol's most-wanted list and was the number one most-wanted person in Canada. When they contacted Canadian police, they got the entire backstory.

———

Albert Johnson Walker was a seemingly successful Canadian businessman living a normal life in Ontario. He ran a financial consulting firm with six branches and taught Sunday school. Then, in 1990, he took his fifteen-year-old daughter, Sheena, on a skiing trip to Europe and left his wife, Barbara, with their three other children. His wife had no idea, but Albert was running away forever and leaving her with a world of problems.

Even though he hadn't finished high school, Walker was a very skilled con man. He had set up his financial consulting firms in the Cayman Islands and had talked his clients, mostly elderly, into investing their retirement savings in his company. Many of them handed over their entire life savings to him. By 1990, he had $3.2 million in cash from over seventy clients when he fled Canada with his daughter in tow.

Provincial police charged him with thirty-two counts of fraud, and he became Canada's most wanted fugitive and number four on Interpol's most wanted list.

Walker originally ended up in Harrogate, North Yorkshire, where he assumed his new identity of David Davis with his daughter, Sheena, posing as his much younger wife. During this time, Sheena had two children. Authorities never revealed the results of paternity tests on the children, but their birth certificates list David Davis as their father.

During his time in Harrogate, he met Elaine Boyes, who was working for a fine art auction house. Elaine told Davis about her boyfriend, Ronald Platt, and their plans to move to Canada. Ronald had always wanted to move to Canada and even had a Canadian maple leaf tattooed on the back of his hand.

Davis offered the couple a job running his new company – The Cavendish Company. He explained that he would like to put the company in their names because he didn't want his ex-wife back in the United States to find out he was making money.

Elaine and Ron agreed and ran his company, often taking trips to other countries where Davis asked them to convert money from Swiss francs to British pounds.

In 1992, Walker surprised Ronald and Elaine with a generous Christmas present. He had purchased them one-way tickets to Calgary, Canada. He knew how much they wanted to move to Canada and gave them the perfect opportunity.

Ronald Platt / Albert Walker / Sheena Davis (Walker)

Amazingly, Walker convinced Ron to leave a rubber stamp of his signature, his driver's license, birth certificate, and a credit card. Walker explained that it was standard operating procedure in those circumstances and that he could continue running the business under their names. With Ron Platt out of the country in Canada, Walker was now free to assume his new identity as Ronald Platt.

His plan worked fine for a few years, but Canada wasn't all Ron had hoped it would be. Finally, he grew tired of the freezing winters and moved back to England. This blew a massive hole in Albert Walker's plan to use Ron's identity, so he decided he would need to get rid of Ron Platt once and for all.

During the trial, Albert Walker pled guilty to defrauding over 70 of his clients of their savings, but he denied killing Ronald Platt.

His daughter, Sheena, testified against her father, claiming she had been "hypnotized" by him. She also admitted the two of them were together in Devon during the time of the murder and had been together every day, except for when he went on the boat with Ronald Platt. After only two hours of deliberation, the jury returned a guilty verdict for both first-degree murder and fraud with a sentence of life in prison.

The clients of Albert Walker could only recover £500,000 of their stolen money; several hundred thousand in gold bars are still missing. After seven years in English prisons, they returned Walker to Canada to face twenty-seven additional fraud, theft, and money laundering charges. In 2021, seventy-five-year-old Walker was denied parole.

CHAPTER 6

PAIGE'S DIRTY LITTLE SECRET

On the afternoon of June 28, 2007, Paige Birgfeld drove two hours from her home in Grand Junction, Colorado, to Eagle, Colorado, for a picnic she had planned with her ex-husband, Howard Beigler. Eagle was the midpoint between Grand Junction and Howard's home in Denver, so it was the perfect meeting point for both of them.

Howard and Paige were high-school sweethearts, but it was a typical story. They fell in love when they were young, and it just didn't work between them, and they divorced after only two years. But now, several years later, there was a lot of water under the bridge. Paige was 34, had three kids, and was divorced for a second time. Nevertheless, she hoped to rekindle some of the romance she and Howard felt when they were young.

Paige's second marriage was to Rob Dixon. Rob came from a very wealthy family that had made their money in the cell phone industry in its infancy, so Rob didn't need to work for a living. Rob had a collection of sports cars including a bright yellow Ferrari and lived in a million-dollar home. When he and Paige first started dating, he showered her with lavish gifts like a $12,000 necklace. So when Rob proposed to her with an $85,000 engagement ring, she couldn't say no.

Rob and Paige had three adorable kids and lived the perfect life, but his demeanor turned when Rob made a string of bad investments, and he showed he had an angry side. During one of their arguments, Paige had to call the police.

> "My husband and I were in a fight, and he was supposed to watch my children while I went to work. He said that I would come home and find them all murdered."

Police filed no charges on that occasion, but the arguments didn't stop. It wasn't long before she called the police again. This time, Rob was arrested for third-degree assault after he had punched and slapped her.

Paige wrote in her blog,

> "My children would ask me if dad was going to kill me. I can't imagine what life would be like for them after he killed me."

When the two divorced after eight years of marriage, Paige gained custody of the kids and kept the house in Grand Junction with its whopping $6,000 per month mortgage payment.

Though stuck with the huge mortgage and not much help from her ex, Paige was determined to make it work. She loved her kids more than anything in the world and turned to her entrepreneurial skills to help support her family. She started a string of dance studios for kids and sold nursing slings for new mothers and cookware through a company called Pampered Chef.

But that Thursday in June, Paige was interested in love. She was hoping there might still be a spark left with her first husband, Howard. The two met for their picnic in Eagle, CO, and that evening, Paige left for the two-hour drive back to Grand Junction.

Paige was due to be home that night, but her kids were terrified when she hadn't arrived by 11 p.m. They got no reply when calling her cell phone. The three children were being watched by their babysitter, who didn't speak English, which only added to the confusion. The poor children, the oldest of which was only eight years old, spent the following day not knowing what had happened and had no idea what to do. The kids finally called Howard in Denver, who told them to have their babysitter take them to the police station and Howard immediately called the Mesa County Sheriff.

Howard told police he had spoken to her around 9 p.m. on Thursday night after their picnic earlier in the day. Paige had called and told him she was just pulling into Grand Junction and had a few people to meet before she went home. However, Howard didn't know whom she was meeting.

That Saturday afternoon, Paige Birgfeld was listed as a missing person, and her family and friends were notified. Of course, the first place to look was with the last person to see Paige, her ex-husband, Howard. He was quickly eliminated as a suspect when phone records showed he spoke with Paige at 9 p.m. that night as she was driving into Grand Junction; he had been on his cell in Denver.

Paige's second ex-husband, Ron, was also an immediate suspect because they'd had such a tumultuous relationship, but he was now living in Pennsylvania and was eliminated as a suspect.

By that evening, over 100 people were searching for her, and police had forensic sniffer dogs were looking for clues. But an ominous clue came that evening from a 911 call to the police. In an empty lot in an industrial part of town, Paige's car was found burning. It was obviously arson. Someone was trying to get rid of evidence.

When police searched the remains of the burned-out car, there were some additional signs of foul play. The driver's side seat was pushed back to its furthest position, yet Paige was only five foot four. With the seat pushed back that far, she wouldn't have even been able to reach the pedals. Someone very tall had been driving her car. Inside the trunk, investigators found Paige's day planner. Though damaged, it had survived the fire and showed that someone had torn out the last four days. Those pages would have shown whom she met that night. Again, someone was destroying evidence.

The forensic dogs tracked a scent at the car and followed it about 500 feet away to a mechanic's shop that serviced RVs, where the scent disappeared.

Despite so many volunteers searching for Paige, the Grand Junction area had vast open spaces. The Colorado River pours into the Gunnison River and twists and turns for hundreds of miles. There were thousands of square miles in which someone could disappear.

Investigators then concentrated their efforts on Paige's last cell phone activity. On the evening that Paige went missing, her last phone call was to Howard. Earlier that day, however, there were calls from another number that wasn't in her contacts. Three calls came in, two went out.

Further investigation of her cell phone revealed that Paige led a secret life that her friends and family didn't know about. There were voicemails left from men asking to meet her in hotel rooms. Besides teaching dance and selling cookware, Paige was selling sex. No one had any idea that the sweet, loving mother of three was secretly running an escort business she called "Models Inc."

When they did further digging, they found photos of Paige – a beautiful, thin, strawberry blonde – listed on escort websites under the name "Carrie." Paige was working as an escort to pay the bills and bring up her three kids by herself.

The police were particularly interested in the five phone calls on Paige's phone from earlier in the day. One message from that number was from a man called Jim.

> "Hello, yeah, this is Jim. Just calling to see if Carrie was available tonight."

Detectives discovered the phone calls came from a "Tracfone," a disposable prepaid cell phone. Only five calls were made to or from the phone – all to Paige's "Models Inc." number.

Tracfones can be somewhat anonymous, but in this instance, police could tell exactly where and what time it had been purchased. It was purchased two days earlier, on June 26, at the local Walmart. Police contacted Walmart and acquired surveillance video taken during the purchase. The footage showed a large white male in his sixties buying the phone.

Upon further investigation, they found that the man's name was Lester Jones, and he worked at "Bob Scott RV," the same RV repair shop just 500 feet from where they found Paige's car in flames.

Paige Birgfeld / Lester Jones

Lester Jones had a prior conviction on his record. In 1999, he was convicted of first-degree sexual assault and kidnapping of his ex-wife. Lester Jones was also a very tall man. At six foot five, Jones would have needed to push a car seat all the way back to drive it.

Police obtained a warrant to search the RV shop where Jones worked. There, they found that Lester Jones had his own secret life under the name of "Jim." During the search, they found packets of Viagra, condoms, and men's toupees. They also found handwritten lists with notes about particular escorts, including their appearances, websites, personalities, types of sex they would perform, and bra sizes. But the most damning two pieces of evidence they found were a gas canister and a food scale made by Pampered Chef, the same company that Paige worked for.

Detectives then took the sniffer dogs back to the burned car, where they found the scent of Lester Jones in the vehicle's front seat.

Police brought Jones into the Sheriff's office for interrogation, but he flatly denied everything. He denied ever meeting

Paige or even knowing who she was. He denied buying the Tracfone and making the calls. When police showed him the surveillance video, he said it wasn't him. Later, he admitted to being at the Walmart during that time but said he was purchasing a Monster Cable, despite the confirmation of the video, receipt, and the clerk remembering selling him the Tracfone.

When asked his whereabouts on Sunday night when Paige's car was found ablaze, he admitted that he had left the house. He claimed that he went back to the RV shop to turn the shop lights off, just 500 feet from where the car was burning. But he claimed he had nothing to do with the burning car – it was just an amazing coincidence.

Despite the seeming mountain of evidence, police had no crime other than the burning car. There was no body. They had no clue whether Paige was dead, or if she was being held somewhere, or if she had just run off on her own accord. Proving he was guilty of anything beyond a reasonable doubt would be a risk. Detectives had no choice but to set Lester Jones free.

———

Two weeks later, on July 16, a motorist traveling on Highway 50 stopped to fix a flat tire. While changing their tire, they noticed a checkbook lying on the side of the road. It was Paige Birgfeld's. Police were notified, and an extensive search of Highway 50 began. Spread all along the highway between Grand Junction and Whitewater, Colorado, they found over two dozen personal items belonging to Paige, such as her Blockbuster Video card, clothing, and her children's medical cards. Police speculated that Paige had been kidnapped and was leaving a trail of breadcrumbs by throwing her personal items out the window of a moving vehicle.

Even with this new evidence, it wasn't enough to bring any charges against Jones. The case went cold and nothing happened for another five years.

———

In the Spring of 2012, about forty miles south of Grand Junction in an area called Wells Gulch, a hiker came across a human skull near the Gunnison River. The flesh around the skull had long since decomposed, but duct tape was still attached to the jawline and back of the head. It was obvious this person had died against their will.

Over the course of almost a year, investigators searched the Gunnison River for more remains. They found bones distributed across a mile of the twisting river. Then, on March 6, 2013, Paige Birgfeld was pronounced dead.

It took another year and a half for prosecutors to put together a case that they believed was strong enough to convict Lester Jones and finally arrested him on November 21, 2014.

Jones' trial started an additional year and a half later in June 2016, but Paige's family was devastated to find that the first trial ended in a mistrial. Nine jurors believed Jones was guilty, but three believed there was reasonable doubt. The prosecuting attorney believed that, because Paige had led a secret life as an escort, some of the jurors may have thought she knew she was putting herself in harm's way and therefore didn't deserve proper justice.

The second trial started the following month. During the trial, Jones' wife testified that he had left the house that Sunday night when the car was found burning. She said that she had often suspected her husband of seeing other women.

As the jury deliberated, they came back with a question. They wanted the prosecution to replay a strange, recorded phone conversation between a police officer and Lester Jones that prosecutors had played earlier.

Sergeant Art Smith had called Jones to return one of his impounded vehicles to him during the investigation when Jones made some odd comments:

Sgt. Smith: "If you need us to bring one to you or come and pick one of you up; we can do that for you."

Lester Jones: "I don't think so."

Sgt. Smith: "Um, Mr. Jones, I'm not following you."

Lester Jones: "You asked me where I would bury a body."

Sgt. Smith: "I'm sorry?"

Lester Jones: "You asked me where I would bury a body."

Sgt. Smith: "When did I ask you that?"

Almost ten years after Paige Birgfeld went missing, the jury finally returned with a verdict. Lester Jones was found guilty on all counts of kidnapping and murder. He was sentenced to life in prison without the possibility of parole.

CHAPTER 7
THE MURDER OF GEORGIA WILLIAMS

Jamie Reynolds seemed like an ordinary young man to his neighbors and schoolmates in Wellington, England. But, he liked to play the role of the heart-broken boy who never got the girl. He posted on social media about how he was "cursed" when it came to girls and how he would be "forever alone." Jamie also had a thing for redheads. One girl in particular, Georgia Williams, caught his eye – but in addition to redheads, he also had a much darker obsession.

Twenty-two-year-old Jamie had a crush on a younger high-school girl named Georgia Williams. Georgia was a bright, vibrant seventeen-year-old redhead who was very active in her school and had been voted "Head Girl," a title similar to "Class President" in US schools. Jamie was in the same class as Georgia's older sister.

Jamie Reynolds / Georgia Williams

On Facebook and ask.fm, Jamie made multiple attempts to get Georgia to become his girlfriend and had once tried to kiss her, but she quickly shot him down. Georgia simply wasn't interested, and she made that clear to him. She liked him as a friend but told him she wasn't interested in having a boyfriend at the time. On April 5, however, when Georgia posted on Facebook that she was in a new relationship, it upset Jamie.

He posted, "Whenever I arrange dates, they either never happen, or the girl magically gains a boyfriend … and it's worse when you actually like someone, your stuck, happy their happy but unhappy coz it's not you."

Jamie thought of himself as an aspiring photographer. At least, that's what he told girls. He devised an elaborate plan to lure Georgia to his home while his parents were on vacation in Italy. Jamie told her he was working on an art project and wanted to recreate a "fake hanging" photo shoot; he needed Georgia to be the model. He told her he wanted it to be an "artistic, floating" image. He assured her that several of her friends would be there watching the photo shoot with them, but that was a lie. She was the only one invited.

Georgia checked with her parents to make sure it was okay.
Her parents knew Reynolds, as he worked at a nearby gas
station and lived only a five-minute walk away. They
thought of him as an ordinary boy from the neighborhood
and, like Georgia, they believed her other friends would be
there too, so they assumed their daughter was safe.

On Sunday, May 26, 2013, Georgia got dressed for the photo
shoot in the clothes Reynolds got for her, told her parents
goodbye, and left. Just as she headed out the door at 7:30
p.m., she got a text from Jamie:

> "I'm so excited. Please don't be late."

That was the last time Georgia's parents saw her alive.

———

At 10:30 that night, when Georgia didn't show up at home,
her mother sent her a text:

> *"Where are you; what are you doing?"*

A text reply came back immediately:

> *"I've left with some friends, going to be out for a while. I'll see you
> later. xxx"*

The "xxx" at the end of her texts was something Georgia
typically added to her texts. They represented kisses—one
for each of her family members.

At 6 a.m. the following morning, when Georgia still hadn't
arrived home, her mother sent her another text. This time,
she didn't get a reply for another two hours:

"I stayed at friends. I'm fine, but my battery is dying too."

Reynolds was playing a cruel joke on her parents. By saying that the battery was "dying too," he was leaving a gruesome hint that Georgia was dying or already dead.

Georgia had planned to attend a music festival that Monday, so her parents didn't think much of her being gone most of the day. They assumed she was with her friends enjoying the festival. It wasn't until the evening, when phone calls to Georgia's phone went unanswered, that her parents became concerned. They started calling her friends, but nobody seemed to know where she was.

Georgia's older sister texted Jamie, but he feigned concern, claiming she had left earlier in the day. He even offered to help look for her.

Georgia had been excited to have her first driving lesson, which was scheduled for Tuesday morning. Her parents definitely knew something was wrong when she hadn't arrived by Tuesday morning, and they finally called the police.

The first thing detectives did was pull a background check of the person she was last seen with, Jamie Reynolds. Just a quick look at his background told a dreadful story. They knew right away she hadn't run away: she had been kidnapped. For only a young man of 22, Reynolds had a dark and disturbing past. Without informing her parents, police rushed to Reynolds' house and broke down the door.

Inside, there was no sign of Georgia or Reynolds, but they noticed his parents' van was missing. Police began a nationwide manhunt across the United Kingdom to find Jamie Reynolds and the van.

When police searched Reynolds' home, they found proof that they were too late. Georgia had already died a horrific death.

Jamie Reynolds

Investigators found memory cards from his digital camera that he attempted to wipe clean, but using recovery software, they were able to recover photos that Reynolds assumed had been erased.

There were photos of Georgia alive with a noose around her neck. Next, photos of her naked dead body. He had hung her in various rooms throughout the house and photographed her. Then he took photos of himself having sex with her lifeless corpse.

The photos showed he dressed her in the clothes he bought for her and restrained her with handcuffs. He then placed a boat oar over two beams in the loft, slung the noose around the oar, and tied the rope's end to the stairs' railing. He then had her stand on a wooden box and put the rope around her neck. Suddenly, he pulled the noose tight and kicked the box out from underneath her. He took photos and watched, all while she kicked and tried to scream as the life drained out of her.

The photos showed that he then laid her dead body on the bed and sexually assaulted her for over an hour. Next, he dragged her body downstairs and positioned it all over the house, taking pictures of himself in sexual positions with the body for several hours.

————

In the early morning hours of Wednesday, May 29, police spotted the van parked outside a Premier Inn just outside of Glasgow, Scotland, almost five hours away from his home. Jamie Reynolds was inside his hotel room when police stormed in and took him into custody.

During the interrogation, Reynolds was cold and emotionless. He refused to help the police in any way whatsoever. Despite the incriminating photo evidence, he refused to admit he murdered Georgia. Instead, he claimed he had no idea where Georgia was and had no recollection of anything. It was an excuse he had used before.

It was clear Reynolds would be no help. Investigators continued searching the house and began retracing his steps, from the day he left Wellington in his parents' van until his arrest in Glasgow.

Investigators located security camera footage of him filling the van with gas, while another camera showed he had stopped in Wrexham, Wales, to watch a movie. He calmly spent a few hours watching Fast & Furious 6, a film he had asked Georgia to see with him. He then stopped at a shopping mall to buy a new watch.

After searching his route, they still found no trace of Georgia, so detectives reached out to the media for help. They hoped they could get additional clues if the public knew what they were looking for. They were in luck.

A witness came forward and said they recognized both the van and Jamie Reynolds. They told detectives that Reynolds' van became stuck in the mud on a country road near a wooded area called Nant-y-Garth Pass, and they had stopped to help him.

Just three days after Georgia was reported missing, the people led police to the area where Reynolds' van was stuck. Nearby, Georgia's body was found naked, unburied in the woods. Reynolds was immediately charged with murder.

Investigators now realized that while the surveillance video showed him pumping gas, Georgia was dead inside the back of the van. She was also in the back of the van as he stopped off to watch the movie.

When police finished their search of Jamie Reynolds' house, they found evidence that he had meticulously planned the murder down to the last detail – and he also planned on doing the same to several other girls. He had even taken the time to answer two calls from other potential victims during his murder of Georgia. Reynolds was a serial killer in the making.

Detectives discovered forty stories he had written that read like a script of his plans for the murders. One was titled "Georgia's Surprise."

During the investigation, detectives found that Reynolds had messaged sixteen young women and invited them to his house that same week to participate in similar photo shoots. They believed he intended to schedule backups, just in case his plans with Georgia didn't work.

When police looked into Reynolds' background, they quickly realized none of this should have happened. Jamie Reynolds had a dangerous obsession with sexual violence against women that should have been given more attention by authorities long before.

In 2008, when he was seventeen, Reynolds attacked a sixteen-year-old redhead girl under similar circumstances. Reynolds lured the girl to his home while his parents were away. He told her he wanted her to pose for photographs for an art project he was working on. When the girl refused to go upstairs with him, he attacked. The girl managed to fight him off, bit him, and broke one of his ribs. Once she escaped, she reported the attack to the police. Unfortunately, they only gave him a "final warning" and counseling.

Two weeks after that incident, Reynolds' parents showed police and his psychiatrist images they had found on his computer. Jamie had a strange obsession with "snuff" films and extreme porn that had started when he was fourteen. He liked to watch films of simulated rape, killing, and necrophilia. He had amassed a collection of 16,800 images and seventy movies of women being asphyxiated, hung, raped, and murdered, including sex with their corpses.

Even more disturbing, Jamie had a collection of photos of girls from his school. He had taken their photos from Facebook and photoshopped nooses around their necks, one of which was Georgia Williams. There were more photos of women being attacked, only he had replaced the faces of the women with the faces of girls from his school. He had even pasted a copy of his own face over the face of each attacker. None of these girls were notified that he had done this.

Even after notifying the police, they told his parents to simply restrict his access to porn. The police had put all the burden upon the parents. But this wasn't your everyday vanilla porn; it was much more sadistic. It was violent porn that depicted simulated rape and torture, which ended in death.

His parents put software blocks on his computer, but Jamie could easily get past those. He installed his own routers in their home so he could fulfill his sick fantasies undetected.

A few years later, in August 2011, Reynolds made advances to a girl where he worked. When he persisted after multiple rejections, she confronted him and told him in no uncertain terms that she wasn't interested. He then got in his car and purposely rammed his car into hers in anger. When he was arrested for Georgia's murder, police found images of this girl on his hard drive with a photoshopped noose around her neck.

Just three months before Georgia Williams' murder, Reynolds had lured another young girl to his home. Another redhead. Again, his parents were out of town. He locked the doors to the house and told her he had lost the keys. He tried to persuade her to stay the night, but she could see through his ruse. She screamed and threatened to break the windows and climb out – at which point he miraculously found the keys and let her go. After Georgia's murder, they found notes he had left himself showing that he'd planned to hang the girl.

The police and social services knew about his deviant intentions, yet Jamie Reynolds was only given warning after warning. Six different agencies were aware of Jamie's dangerous obsessions but did nothing to stop him. If police and social services had coordinated information, registered him earlier as a sex offender, and monitored his actions, Georgia Williams may have known of his background, and her life may have been spared.

Over the next six months, Reynolds said nothing and Georgia's family assumed they would have to go through a long and difficult trial. However, just five days before the trial's start date, Reynolds finally submitted a guilty plea. The judge, however, showed no leniency. Due to his potential to become a serial killer, Jamie Reynolds was sentenced to a full-life sentence, meaning he will never be released. This is a very rare sentence in the UK, with only about 100 offenders serving a full-life sentence – Jamie Reynolds is among the youngest.

CHAPTER 8

THE GIRL IN THE BOX

In 1977, hitchhiking in the United States was a common mode of transportation, even for young girls. Colleen Stan was a free-spirited twenty-year-old girl hitchhiking her way from Eugene, Oregon, to the small Northern California town of Westwood to surprise a friend for her birthday. After accepting rides with truckers traveling south on Interstate 5, she made her way to Red Bluff, California, where she needed to change onto Highway 36.

She turned down a few rides while waiting at the on-ramp to Highway 36. They just looked like they could be trouble. Then, finally, a couple stopped to offer her a ride: Cameron and Janice Hooker. At first glance, they seemed to be a normal enough couple. Safe. Cameron looked a bit nerdy with his big seventies-style eyeglasses, and Janice held a two-month-old baby in her arms. Colleen accepted the ride.

During the drive, there was almost no conversation at all – but Cameron kept glancing at her in the rear-view mirror, which made Colleen a bit uneasy. When they stopped at a gas station, Colleen took the opportunity to use the restroom. Something inside her felt she should find another ride, but she was so close to her destination; she decided to continue riding with the couple.

A bit further down the road, Cameron asked if it was okay if they made a stop to see some ice caves just off the main highway. Colleen said she didn't mind. She wasn't in a hurry.

They drove down a dirt road, stopped, and the couple walked to a creek bed while Colleen remained in the car. She had lost sight of the couple when Cameron suddenly jumped into the car's back seat with her. He grabbed her arms and threw her face down onto the back seat. He handcuffed her wrists, blindfolded her, and shoved a gag into her mouth. He then forced her head into a large wooden box.

The wooden box was a homemade bondage device called a sensory deprivation head box. It was large and heavy, with two sides hinged together at the top like a clamshell. It had a hole at the bottom just big enough to fit around her neck. The inside of the box was coated with carpet to muffle her screams. Colleen was lying helpless in the back seat as they continued driving down Highway 36.

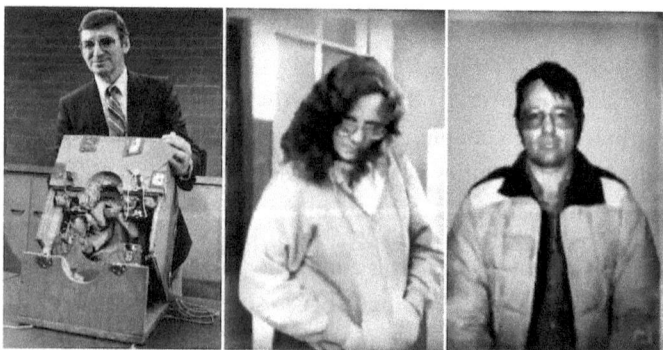

Deprivation head box / Janice Hooker / Cameron Hooker

When the car finally stopped, Cameron removed the box from her head and led her into a house, then the basement. He removed her clothes and left her blindfolded. Cameron forced Colleen to stand on a metal ice chest and raise her arms. He bound her wrists with leather restraints connected to hooks on a ceiling beam. He then pulled out the ice chest from beneath her, leaving her suspended from the ceiling by her wrists. He then whipped her back with a leather whip while she dangled, kicking and screaming.

As Cameron whipped her, she could see through a gap in her blindfold. On a counter nearby, she saw glimpses of a magazine with a photo of a woman strapped up exactly like she was. He was acting out his fantasy from a BDSM magazine. He then let her rest her toes on a box while he and Janice had sex as they looked at her.

Colleen's screams only encouraged him. He howled back at her,

> "Go ahead and scream! I'll cut your vocal cords out! I've done it before!"

She believed him, and it may have actually been true. The year prior, a young girl in the area named Marie Spannhake went missing. Janice later revealed that she and Cameron had kidnapped her as well, although Cameron couldn't control himself: he killed her after only one day in captivity.

Colleen's torture continued for hours, until he finally let her sit naked on the ice chest. Cameron then put the wooden sensory deprivation box back on her head, laid her in a larger wooden box about the size of a coffin, chained her wrists together, and tied her feet to the inside corners of the box.

Cameron Hooker had been busy building homemade bondage devices and preparing for his victim. The following day, he put Colleen on another device he called "the rack." He chained her wrists and ankles to the corners of the rack and left her until the next day.

On the third day, Cameron tried to feed Colleen, but she couldn't keep her food down and threw up everything she ate. This only angered him, so he hung her by her wrists and whipped her more. When he finished, he attached her to the rack again.

———

Later that week, Colleen's roommates were getting worried when they heard she hadn't shown up at her friend's house. They called her family in Riverside, California, and the family began searching for her. They drove 900 miles north to Eugene, stopping at every town along the way to report Colleen missing. Sadly, they found no clues and returned to Riverside.

Cameron kept Colleen naked, chained to the rack, and wearing the head box for the entire first week. Over the next five months, he kept Colleen naked in the box in the basement. She was gagged, blindfolded, bound, and forced to wear the head box. Once every evening Cameron allowed her to urinate, defecate, eat, and drink, but always as he watched.

During these first several months, he allowed her out of the box only for his sadistic pleasures. He whipped her, choked her, shocked her, and burned her genitals with a heat lamp. He also held her head underwater in the bathtub to the edge of drowning. Colleen later recalled that Cameron Hooker hung and whipped her at least 90 times during these first six months – but he was just getting started.

In October 1977, Cameron built another box in which to hold his slave. It was a triangular shape that wedged neatly beneath the stairs, which he called "the workshop." Colleen spent the next six months chained and locked inside the workshop. She was only allowed out for his bondage pleasures and occasionally to do chores around the house.

Cameron built yet another device he called "the stretcher," which pulled Colleen's arms and legs taut and stretched. Unfortunately, over time, this device caused permanent damage to her back and shoulder.

Cameron Hooker's mental manipulation of Colleen really took effect when he told her of an underground organization of slave owners called "The Company." According to Hooker, The Company was a powerful organization that closely watched all her movements. Their members were everywhere. Any slaves caught attempting to escape were taken from their current masters and sold to other masters – masters that could be much crueler than he was being to her. She believed his story, but it was all just a work of fiction that he had read about in one of his bondage porn magazines.

Over the subsequent years, he expanded on The Company story, making her more and more frightened of them. When his wife, Janice, had knee surgery and came home with a bandage on her knee, Cameron explained to Colleen that Janice had once been a slave who had tried to escape. He said The Company had tortured her for trying to escape and permanently damaged her legs.

The truth was that Janice was never a slave; she was Cameron's wife. She had undoubtedly endured his sexual sadism, but not to the extreme that Colleen was currently experiencing.

Janice, however, didn't enjoy his perverted exploits. She wanted some semblance of a normal life and desperately wanted to have another baby. She also didn't want her husband to have sex with another woman. So, Janice and Cameron came to an agreement: she could have a baby, and he could have his slave. But there was one stipulation. He was not to have sex with his slave. He could whip and torture her, but sex was reserved for his wife exclusively.

Colleen's enslavement went through several stages, and in January 1978, a new stage began. It involved a contract. Cameron created a "Slave Contract" that he presented to Colleen. The contract was an official document stating that she was his slave and that he owned her soul. But, again, it was actually something he'd seen in a bondage magazine. Colleen initially refused to sign it, but Cameron explained that a representative of The Company was waiting for the signed contract; she reluctantly agreed.

Once Colleen had signed the contract, he changed her name to her slave name, "Kay." She was to address Hooker as "Sir" or "Master," and she was to call Janice "Ma'am." The contract also required her to bow, kneel, and ask permission before doing anything at all. In addition, a leather collar with a steel ring was placed around her neck to be worn at all times, so she would never forget she was a slave. He also pierced her labia, another symbol of her enslavement.

Although Cameron had agreed with Janice to not have sex with his slave, it was Janice that first suggested he have sex with her. She thought it might excite her if she watched him raping her. It didn't. It only sparked her jealousy. It was also the start of many more rapes to come.

Internally, Colleen retreated to the confines of her mind. She learned that she could do anything and be anywhere in her mind. It was the only way she could cope. Colleen cried every day but never let Cameron see her crying because she knew it would anger him.

In April 1978, the Hookers moved from their small house into a mobile home on an acre of land nearby. This began the third stage of Colleen's enslavement. Cameron built a new box for Colleen in the new mobile home that doubled as the pedestal for their waterbed. Colleen lived in a small box just beneath where they slept and had sex. He only allowed her a bedpan, some toilet paper, and a radio in her new box. She spent most of each day and night in confinement beneath the bed, to be let out only once for a few minutes each night.

In September 1978, Janice gave birth to their second child. The baby was born on the waterbed while Colleen was locked in the box below.

Janice got a night job the following year, while Cameron worked days. In Janice's absence, he let Colleen out of her box in the evenings to do chores and make dinner for her master.

By June 1980, Cameron knew that the fear of The Company was enough to keep Colleen in line – which meant that, when Janice got a daytime job, they allowed Colleen to babysit the two children by herself. This started yet another stage. Out of fear that The Company was always watching, she didn't run. She believed that, if she were caught, she would be tracked down, tortured, and possibly even killed. Cameron had also told her they would kill her family.

During this stage of her enslavement, Colleen was allowed to sleep in the back bathroom while chained to the toilet. The two children had no idea that Colleen even lived in the same house.

By February 1981, Cameron wanted Colleen back in the box he had built under the waterbed, but Janice said she would work from home to watch over Colleen instead. During this time, Colleen was allowed much more freedom. Still, The Company's threat loomed over her, so she stayed compliant and didn't attempt to escape.

Colleen was permitted to work for Janice's employer assembling electronics at home, but the paychecks were all handed over to Cameron. She was also required to help Cameron dig a large hole in the property's yard. The hole was lined with concrete blocks and took two years to build.

Cameron had big plans for the hole that he hadn't told Janice. It was to be "The Dungeon," and he would build a shed over it to house more slaves. He had established his power over Janice and now had plans to abduct four more slaves.

By 1980, three years had passed. Colleen knew Cameron had no intention of killing her, but she also knew that she would never get out of her horrible enslavement. This was now how her life would be – forever. Hoping Cameron may treat her better, Colleen told him she loved him and wrote him love letters:

> "I seem to be falling deeper and deeper in love with you with each passing day."

"Sometimes, I feel that being your slave has made me more of a woman. But then there are other times when I feel it has made me less of a woman. You know how to make me feel good about myself, and I love you so much for it."

"My love for you is growing with every changing day. You fill my life with happiness and love. And I pray that that happiness and love will never end."

———

Colleen begged Cameron several times to allow her to contact her family, just to let them know she was okay. Writing the love letters to him may have actually paid off. After almost four years of confinement, Cameron felt confident in his control over her. He knew she was terrified of The Company and would do what she was told, so he granted her a phone call – but made sure she knew that The Company was listening. Her family would be tortured or killed if she made the slightest mistake or said the wrong thing.

By this time, her family had completely lost hope of ever finding her alive. When she called, her youngest sister, Bonnie, answered the phone. Colleen gave no details but let her know that she was alive and well, then she said her goodbyes.

The family didn't contact the police. Instead, they were happy that she was alive but still left with many unanswered questions. They assumed she had become a member of a cult, which was common in California at that time.

Cameron Hooker enjoyed letting Colleen talk to her family and allowing her bits of freedom. It gave him reassurance that she wouldn't run; it proved that he had ultimate control over her. By February 1981, he told her that he would take her to visit her family the following month. He claimed he had to pay a $30,000 deposit to The Company to cover the extra costs of watching her and her family during the visit.

Before the trip, however, he asked Colleen to prove her obedience. He handed her a gun and told her to put it in her mouth, then pull the trigger. She did as she was told. Luckily, the gun wasn't loaded.

Just as he had promised, Hooker took Colleen to Riverside – but on the drive south, they stopped at "The Company Headquarters." Hooker told Colleen that The Company required her to pass a lie detector test before she could visit her family. She was extremely frightened to meet someone from The Company. Finally, they arrived at a building in Sacramento, and Cameron went inside, while Colleen sat in the car. When he returned, he claimed that he had talked them into waiving the test requirement, and they continued on their drive.

Colleen visited with her family, and Hooker posed as her boyfriend. He told the family that he had a computer seminar in San Diego and would be back later to pick her up.

Now that she was finally alone with her family, she wanted to let them know the whole truth, but she worried for her own safety and that of her family. She knew The Company was always watching. Colleen stayed overnight with her family, and Cameron picked her up the next day.

Colleen Stan / Colleen posing with Cameron while visiting her family

When Cameron and Colleen returned to Red Bluff, Janice wasn't home. So, he raped her and put her in the box beneath the waterbed.

Cameron often made Janice read the Bible to him. He chose particular passages for her to read that mentioned wives and slaves and how they were required to be submissive. Janice was devoutly religious and deeply feared hell; she believed that if she didn't obey her husband, she would be damned to the eternal torture of hell.

Near the end of 1983, Cameron put Colleen in the hole she had dug in the backyard. She was there day and night and was not to come out despite the heavy rains turning the hole into several inches of mud. She was there for a week, until Cameron suspected a boy from the neighborhood might have wandered into the backyard and seen her. He brought her back inside and put her back in the box under the bed.

Cameron had grown much more trusting of his power over Colleen and gradually allowed her increasingly more free-dom. By January 1984, he let Colleen out of the box at night and sometimes slept in the back bedroom. He allowed her to run in the neighborhood for exercise and occasionally ride a bicycle. By May, she began working as a maid at a local hotel in Red Bluff, while Cameron kept all the money she earned. All the while, she knew that The Company was still watching every move she made. Janice had also been attending church regularly and Cameron sometimes allowed Colleen to go with her.

July 1984 marked yet another change. Cameron became much more demanding of both women. He decided he wanted to have sex with Janice while fondling Colleen and vice versa. He broke his agreement with Janice and told her he would have sex with both of them on alternating nights. Neither Janice nor Colleen liked the idea but felt they had to obey.

In August 1984, when Cameron told Janice of his plans to abduct four more slaves, it deeply upset her. She was already agitated that he was having sex with Colleen and didn't like the idea of sharing him even more.

On August 9, Janice dropped Colleen off at work, checked into a hotel, and then went to church to speak with her pastor. She opened up completely to him and told the pastor the horrid story; the pastor advised that she and Colleen run away from her husband. Janice then picked up Colleen and returned to the hotel, where she told her for the first time that there was no such thing as The Company. It was all a lie. Colleen was distraught that she had believed the threat so wholeheartedly.

The following day, Janice and Colleen took the two children to Janice's parents' house, where Colleen called her family. Her father arranged to wire money for bus fare home. Before she left, Colleen called Cameron and told him she knew there was no such thing as The Company and that he no longer had power over her. Cameron cried on the phone.

Janice tried to stay away, but after only a week, moved back in with Cameron. She took him to church with her and encouraged him to attend counseling. Together, they destroyed many of the bondage items over the next month, but Janice hid some things. For several weeks, Janice suffered debilitating anxiety attacks and was unable to eat or sleep. On September 28, she left her husband again and moved back in with her parents.

In the months after Colleen left, she communicated with Janice and Cameron on the telephone and through letters. Janice begged her not to go to the police, saying she was trying to get help for Cameron. Colleen initially agreed, but her family pressured her to contact the authorities. Nevertheless, Colleen was grateful just to be alive and have her freedom back.

Janice was still terrified of Cameron and worried that he would hurt her or the children. Eventually, at the suggestion of her pastor, Janice contacted the police.

———

When a woman comes into a police station and claims that she and her husband had kidnapped a young woman, kept her as a slave, and tortured her for seven years, it's a little hard to believe. Initially, detectives didn't know what to think and doubted her story – but after traveling to Riverside to speak to Colleen, they knew her story was true. Police arrested Cameron Hooker for kidnapping with the use of a deadly weapon, three counts of imprisonment, seven counts of forcible rape, two counts of abduction for illicit relations, and single counts of forcible sodomy, forcible oral copulation, and penetration with a foreign object. He brazenly pled not guilty to all charges.

At trial, the prosecution produced over 100 pieces of evidence including the head box, photos that Cameron had taken of Colleen on the rack and in bondage, and a copy of the slavery contract. They rebuilt the entire waterbed pedestal and the stretcher inside the courtroom for the jury to see. The prosecution even invited jury members to lie inside the box to see what it was like – and some accepted.

Hooker admitted that he kidnapped Colleen but claimed that, in the later years, she was free to go anytime she liked and had plenty of opportunities to leave. The defense also presented the love letters that Colleen had written to Hooker and a photo of Colleen at her family's house, smiling as she wrapped her arms around Cameron. He also claimed all of their sex was consensual.

Both the prosecution and the defense brought in psychologists. The prosecution's psychologist believed Colleen was coerced by the fear of The Company and was unable to leave. The defense psychologist believed the exact opposite.

The jury found Hooker guilty of ten felony counts – all but one charge. The last charge of rape resulted in a hung jury.

Prosecutors never brought charges for the murder of Marie Spannhake against Hooker due to lack of evidence.

The judge sentenced Cameron Hooker to 95 years in prison and a $50,000 fine. In return for her testimony against Cameron, Janice Hooker wasn't charged and now lives in California under a different name.

Colleen Stan has appeared on several television shows, and a Lifetime movie was made of her story. Watching her on television years later, she seems to have endured the ordeal amazingly well.

CHAPTER 9
THE GREEN CHAIN KILLER

L ondon is known as the greenest city in Europe, with over 3,000 parks covering more than 35,000 acres. The Green Chain Walk was a series of trails that spanned over fifty miles and connected many of the parks on London's south side. Locals used the areas to exercise, walk dogs, and sunbathe, and many young mothers visited with their children.

During the late eighties and early nineties, a string of rapes and murders along the Green Chain terrified London residents. Sadly, the murders were allowed to continue due to blind reliance on a single criminal profile and gross mishandling of police work on several different levels.

───

In August 1989, a young mother in Southeast London was in her home near Plumstead Common park. It was a warm summer morning, and she had left her back door open to let the air in while she got her kids ready for school. Suddenly, she saw a man standing in her doorway with a knife. The woman was brutally raped in front of her children but escaped with her life. Her children were unharmed.

Three months later, Pauline Lasham called the police and told them that her son, Robert Napper, had confessed to her that he had raped a woman in Plumstead Common, near their home. Police searched their records, however, and found no rapes in the park during that time. The rape in August happened in the woman's home - not on Plumstead Common - so no connection was made, and nothing further was done.

Robert Napper was twenty-three years old, suffered from Asperger's syndrome, and was later diagnosed with paranoid schizophrenia. As a child, he frequently watched his father beat his mother until their divorce, when he was nine years old. After the divorce, he and his siblings were placed in foster care, and Robert received psychiatric treatment for the next six years.

On a camping trip at age twelve, Robert Napper was sexually abused by a family friend. The trauma led to a change in Robert and ignited his journey into violence. In his early teens, he shot his brother in the face with an air gun and secretly watched his sister undressing. In school, Robert was a social outcast to an extreme. In a game of English football, if he headed the ball then the game stopped. None of the other children wanted to play after the ball had touched his head. His first brush with the police was when he was nineteen and caught carrying a loaded handgun in public. His only punishment was a fine of £10.

———

In March 1992, there were two more rapes along the Green Chain in Southeast London. A third rape, this time of a young mother walking her daughter in a stroller, occurred just months later in the same area.

From witness reports, police developed a composite sketch of the suspect that looked similar to Robert Napper. Several of his neighbors had reported him as a possible suspect in the Green Chain rapes, and police brought him in for questioning.

During questioning, detectives asked Napper to submit his DNA, but twice he didn't show up for his appointment. Police never followed up on his missed appointments, and he was later dismissed as a suspect strictly based on his height. Robert Napper was six foot four; the descriptions of the rapist were of someone shorter, so they promptly crossed him off their list of suspects.

Fifteen miles away in Southwest London was another park called Wimbledon Common. On the morning of July 15, 1992, a young mother named Rachel Nickell was walking with her two-year-old son, Alex, through a wooded area of the park. In broad daylight, with nearly 500 people in the park, Rachel was attacked and raped at knifepoint. The attacker stabbed her forty-nine times, slashing her throat to near decapitation. Her son, just shy of his third birthday, watched in horror.

Minutes later, an older man found the little boy trying to wake his mother, but Rachel Nickell was already beyond help. He alerted the police, who immediately closed off the park and questioned everyone they could find.

———

Colin Stagg was a thirty-year-old man that lived near Wimbledon Common and frequently walked his dog through the park. But that Wednesday morning, police stopped Colin as he entered the park. They informed him that there had been an incident, and they weren't letting people into the park. Colin mentioned that he had already been in the park earlier that morning, so officers took his name and address, and he returned home.

The crime scene was horribly bloody, but the police were left with almost no evidence. There was just a tiny speck on her body that may have contained DNA, but in 1992, DNA evidence was still relatively new. Unfortunately, they weren't able to get any clues from it. A month after the killing, police had interviewed over 100 people but were still no closer to an answer of who killed Rachel Nickell, other than a few sketches of someone that people in the park said looked suspicious.

Police recruited a criminal psychologist named Paul Britton to create a psychological profile of what traits the killer could have. Britton was known for working on other high-profile cases and had already been working on the Green Chain rapes. However, neither Britton nor the police saw any link between the Rachel Nickell murder and the Green Chain rapes on the other side of London.

Paul Britton developed a profile of the killer. He believed the killer was twenty to thirty years old, a loner with isolated hobbies, most likely lived alone near Wimbledon Common, may have an obsession with knives, may have knowledge or interest in the occult, saw women as sexual objects, and was sexually sadistic.

Rachel Nickell was a beautiful, blonde model. Because she was murdered with her young son watching, the media put enormous pressure on the police to find the killer. The profile presented by Britton was released to television stations, and the police received several calls naming one man: Colin Stagg.

When police arrived at Colin's home, he openly welcomed them in. He had no prior arrests, but police believed he fit their psychological profile. He lived alone and near the park, was a bit of a loner, was thirty years old, and they found a book about the occult on his bookshelf.

Colin Stagg was arrested and brought in for further inter-views. He had been arrested before for sunbathing nude in the same park, but the area had been a popular spot among nude sunbathers. However, detectives believe he was respon-sible for the murder of Rachel Nickell. As they had no evidence and only suspicion, they had to release him after three days.

When the news of Colin's arrest reached the media, the police received a call from a woman named Julie Pines. Julie had met Colin through a dating advertisement, and the two exchanged letters. As their letters grew into a sexual nature, Colin told her of his fantasy to have sex in the open air. She still had the letter and presented it to the police. Again, this reaffirmed to the police that Colin was the killer.

Police then went out on a limb and, under Paul Britton's supervision, developed an elaborate plan they code-named "Operation Edzell." Over the next twenty-eight months, detectives enlisted an undercover female police officer named Lizzy James. Lizzy posed as a friend of Julie Pines and sent Colin letters saying she was much more open-minded than her friend Julie.

Colin had never been with a woman at the time and was quite innocent in his replies to Lizzy. She wrote raunchy letters laced with sexual innuendo, but his replies were naïve, romantic letters, saying how he would like to sip parsnip wine with her on a veranda. Detectives needed more, so they had Lizzy push him.

She wrote to him,

> "I'm sure your fantasies hold no bounds, and you are as broad-minded and uninhibited as I am."

Colin replied with near-verbatim responses, also saying that his fantasies held no bounds.

Eventually, she escalated the conversation, telling him of relationships she had with other men,

> "The things that happened when I was with this man are not what normal people would like. And even though these things are bad, and I feel guilty, I can never forget how exhilarating they make me feel. I need to feel defenseless and humiliated."

Colin, just wanting to be with a woman for the first time, replied with what he believed she wanted to hear.

Lizzy continued to make the letters more sexual and increasingly violent. Eventually, detectives decided to have Lizzy meet Colin in person while undercover officers watched nearby. They met in a coffee shop where Lizzy told him of her dark secret. She told Colin that her prior boyfriend was into black magic and that the two of them had once murdered a pregnant woman as a human sacrifice. Colin thought she was a bit crazy but played along, listening to her stories and saying nothing incriminating.

By the third meeting, she pushed him to open up. He admitted to her that he had been arrested for the Rachel Nickell murder but told her he didn't do it. That excited her; she said she would have sex with the man that *had* committed that murder. But that was over the limit for Colin, and he told her, "No, I'm sorry, it's not me."

Throughout all the contact with Lizzy, Colin never suggested that he had anything to do with the murder of Rachel Nickell, but that didn't deter the police. They were convinced that the wording of the letters matched the psychological profile developed by Paul Britton. On August 17, 1993, Colin Stagg was arrested again on suspicion of murdering Rachel Nickell. After spending two years with Operation Edzell and £3 million in the process, police wholeheartedly believed they had their man.

Meanwhile, rapes continued along the Green Chain, but detectives and prosecutors still refused to believe the murder of Rachel Nickell and these rapes were linked.

Three months after the arrest, with Colin still sitting in jail awaiting trial, another murder occurred in Plumstead, Southeast London.

Samantha Bissett and her four-year-old daughter, Jazmine Bissett, were brutally murdered in their home. Samantha was butchered with a knife, and parts of her body were cut off and taken as a trophy. Her daughter was raped and smothered to death.

A third investigation team was assigned to this case, separate from the Green Chain investigation team. Again, Paul

Britton was brought in as a criminal profiler, but he never once said that he believed any of the crimes were linked.

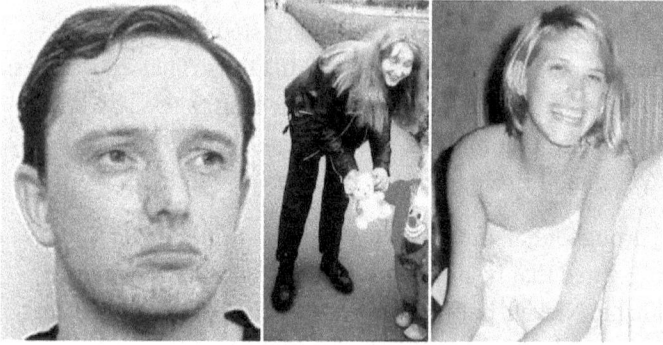

Robert Napper / Samantha Bissett / Rachel Nickell

The Rachel Nickell murder squad was invited to go over the Plumstead murder evidence, but they denied the offer. They were convinced they already had their man behind bars, and there was no need to look any further.

At the Bissett crime scene, investigators found Robert Napper's fingerprints on the outside balcony and a bloody shoe print in the kitchen that matched shoes found at Napper's home.

They had acquired Robert Napper's fingerprints after he was arrested in October 1992 for impersonating a police officer and possessing a firearm. During that arrest, police found a map book in his flat. He had pages meticulously marked and annotated with comments about violent acts and abuse towards women. The marks on the map pointed to several locations along the Green Chain, but investigators still made no links to the Green Chain rapes.

Robert Napper's fingerprints were also found on a knife buried in Wimbledon Common just 100 yards from where Rachel was murdered, but the Rachel Nickell team ignored this evidence.

Colin Stagg, meanwhile, was still sitting in jail awaiting trial. After fourteen months in jail, a judge took one look at how the police had coaxed Stagg into his statements and threw out the case against him. The judge was disgusted with their coercive tactics, calling their undercover work a "Honey Trap." Although Colin Stagg was released from jail and all charges against him dropped, the court of public opinion had already convicted him. His life would never be the same.

Colin was free in the eyes of the law but not in the eyes of the media and the public, who pegged him as someone who got away with murder rather than someone who was found not guilty. He was met by angry mobs outside the courthouse chanting, "Hang him!" and "Guilty!"

Even Rachel Nickell's father believed they had let a guilty man go. He made a statement to the media,

> "I understand that the police will now keep the files on my daughter's murder open, but they are not looking for anyone else. The law has been upheld, but where is the justice?"

Investigators in the Rachel Nickell murder had wasted over three years and £3 million chasing an innocent man, but they still refused to admit they were wrong.

———

In November 1995, Robert Napper pleaded guilty to manslaughter in the Bissett case and admitted guilt in only one rape and two attempted rapes. He admitted nothing regarding the Rachel Nickell murder or the many other rapes along the Green Chain.

Ultimately, Robert Napper claimed "diminished responsibility" and was sentenced to indefinite detention at Broadmoor, a high security hospital for the criminally insane.

For the next seven years, police and Rachel Nickell's family still believed that Colin Stagg had gotten away with murder. In 2002, however, they assigned a case review team to go through the cold case in much more detail. A fresh set of eyes. All witness statements, known offenders, and possible suspects were looked into, including Robert Napper. By that time, there had been considerable advances in DNA research. When they re-examined Rachel's jogging pants, they found a small amount of Robert Napper's DNA. They also found a tiny fleck of red paint in her son's hair that forensically matched a toolbox that Robert Napper owned. This pinned the murder on Robert Napper, who was already serving indefinite detention.

This also finally eliminated Colin Stagg as a suspect, who filed a formal complaint against Paul Britton. Britton was ultimately cleared of seven counts of misconduct, but Colin Stagg was awarded £706,000 for being the victim of a miscarriage of justice. Colin Stagg received a formal public apology from the police, but Paul Britton refused to apologize. Colin says that to this day, some people still think he murdered Rachel Nickell.

Lizzy James was awarded £125,000, claiming that her undercover work on this case ruined her career.

Ultimately, this case led to considerable changes in how investigations are handled in the United Kingdom.

In total, Robert Napper is believed to have been responsible for 106 attacks across London throughout the late eighties and early nineties.

CHAPTER 10

THE MURDER OF NICOLE LEGER

Nicole Leger had some difficulties earlier in life. At seventeen, she was a stunning beauty but unmarried and pregnant. To make ends meet after her son was born, she danced in a few strip clubs around the Dallas area. By the time she was in her thirties, however, things were looking up. Her son was in high school and she was working as an assistant for a stockbroker. She enrolled in nursing school and had just met a wonderful man who treated her like an angel. That man was Mike Adams.

Mike was sixteen years older than Nicole and made his living as a repo man, repossessing cars when people couldn't make their payments. His business did quite well and he owned a lovely new home in the affluent Dallas suburb of Frisco, Texas. When Mike and Nicole first started dating, he was a perfect gentleman who brought her flowers and wrote her love notes.

It wasn't long before Mike asked Nicole and her son, Trey, to move in with him. The bliss, however, didn't last long, and the relationship fell apart quickly.

Mike was obsessive with his personal belongings and his home. He took pride in meticulously maintaining his luxurious house. Items in the closets, cupboards, and refrigerator were all perfectly organized to the point that labels on cans had to be facing the same direction, as if they were on a supermarket display. Even the pool table was strictly a showpiece, never to be used. It was the same with the fancy circular white couch. Worried that it might get dirty, Mike forbade anyone from sitting on it. Order and uniformity were important to Mike; even his extensive handgun collection was sorted by caliber size.

One evening Mike made spaghetti for Nicole, knowing it was her favorite dish. But when Trey spilled a bit of sauce on the tile floor, Mike blew a gasket. A simple spill that was easily cleaned up created a yelling spree that lasted for over a week.

Nicole Leger

Less than two months after Nicole and her son moved in, they moved out. The yelling was just more than Nicole could handle.

Mike wasn't used to being left by a woman, so he turned the charm back on and asked Nicole if he could treat her to dinner at a nice restaurant. During their meal, he fell over himself apologizing and swore he would never yell at her again. Mike was back to a perfect gentleman.

After dinner and a delightful evening, he took Nicole back to his house and asked her to marry him. Nicole couldn't resist the big diamond ring and, unfortunately, couldn't see through his fake charm. She accepted his proposal, and they decided that she would move back in.

Of course, the arguments started again almost immediately – and they escalated. The yelling got so heated that Mike forcefully ripped the ring from Nicole's finger during an argument, requiring a trip to the hospital for a fractured finger.

Nicole and her son moved out again, got a new apartment across town, and tried to put the past behind them. Unfortunately, life would not return to normal for Nicole.

She came home from work one evening to find the front door wide open and their dog missing. A few days later, they learned a car had hit the dog, and it had died. Another day, Nicole came home to find someone had broken into their home and poured bleach all over her clothes. Finally, her car mysteriously caught fire while parked outside their apartment. Nicole suspected Mike was behind all of these anomalies, but she had no way to prove it.

She couldn't afford a new car on her own, so Mike used the opportunity to come to the rescue and offer to cosign on a loan for a new car. She believed she had no choice and accepted his offer.

In March 2013, Nicole took the car title to Mike's house. She wanted him to sign off on the title so the car would be all hers and she would finally be done with him. She wanted Mike out of her life and also needed to pick up some of the belongings she had left there.

Mike again turned on the charm and offered to make spaghetti for her, knowing she couldn't resist a nice plate of pasta. He claimed he was trying to make peace, but peace was the last thing on his mind.

It didn't take long for the knockout drug to take effect. Mike had spiked the spaghetti sauce, incapacitating her for a few hours.

The drug took some time for full effect, and Nicole remembered being walked into the bedroom and Mike taking her clothes off.

"I'm saying no, but I can't do anything. I can't move my arms or legs," Nicole later told the police.

Mike bent Nicole over and inserted a large sex toy into her. They had never used sex toys when they were a couple. Mike then started taking pictures of her with the dildo inside her. Then she passed out completely.

When Nicole woke up, she was hog-tied in the bedroom, still naked. Her hands were tied behind her back, and her ankles were tied together. She was unable to scream because her mouth was gagged with duct tape.

She managed to get herself untied and ran naked from the house to the nearest neighbor's house, screaming and banging on the door. But Mike heard her screams before the neighbors did, grabbed her, and dragged her back into his garage.

Mike put down a large plastic tarp on the floor in the garage, handcuffed her, and bound her ankles with zip ties. His anger consumed him. He tried ripping her hair out, but he couldn't get it to come out – so he cut her hair using a knife.

After being held captive for a full twenty-four hours, Nicole realized the only way she would get out of this alive was to reason with him. She promised she wouldn't press charges if he let her go and vowed they would stay together and go to couple's counseling. It took time, but Mike finally agreed and released her.

Nicole immediately went to the hospital and reported the assault to the police. She pleaded with them to lock him up. They let her know that she would have to testify against him. "He's going to end up killing me," she told the investigators.

Police searched Mike's house and car. He had planned on getting rid of the evidence, but he wasn't quick enough. They found what they were looking for in the trunk of the car — the sex toy, the zip ties, and duct tape with her hair still attached. They even found the near-empty jar of spiked spaghetti sauce.

Detective Scott Greer was in charge of her case. Police arrested Mike on charges of aggravated sexual assault and unlawful restraint, but he quickly made bail and was a free man awaiting trial. Because of his release, Nicole was granted an emergency protective order against him. Mike was to have no contact with her at all.

Nicole and her son moved twenty miles away to Melissa, Texas, in another county. She used a friend's name to rent a home and set up her utilities in hopes it would keep Mike from finding her.

Her hopes were vanquished when Mike sent flowers to her home. She didn't understand how, but he had found her. Nicole filed another police complaint, as this clearly violated her protective order. She told the police,

"I feel like he will show up at my door or car at any time."

Her complaint to the police only angered Mike more. One day, she came home from work to find a plastic tarp and handcuffs on her front porch. This was obviously a not-so-subtle threat from Mike. He didn't want her to testify against him.

Nicole and her son were terrified. In August 2013, they visited her father in Florida to get away for a while. He pleaded with her to stay with him there and told her there was nothing worth returning to Texas for, but Nicole didn't listen. That was the last time her father saw her.

On September 9, 2013, Nicole's seventeen-year-old son returned home from school to find his mother dead. Nicole's body lay face-down and naked on her bed with two gunshot wounds to her face.

Working for an auto repossession company, Mike had used a GPS tracking device that he attached to her car to track her every move.

Police promptly arrested Mike Adams and charged him with capital murder, a term used only in seven states. It meant the crime was eligible for the death penalty.

Crime scene investigators recovered two used condoms at the scene. Both had DNA that didn't match Mike or anyone in police databases, but the outside of one condom matched Mike's DNA. Clearly, he had tried to plant evidence.

Police also saw on his work computers that he had been tracking her using the GPS and had searched for routes to her home in Melissa, Texas.

Mike Adams / Nicole Leger

The most damning evidence, however, was a storage locker in his ex-wife's name. There they found a massive arsenal of guns, one of which ballistically proved to be the gun that fired the two slugs into Nicole's face.

However, it was revealed during the trial that Nicole and Detective Greer, the officer with whom she filed the first complaint, had exchanged sexual texts. A search of Greer's cell phone showed Nicole had been sending the detective nude photos of herself.

Greer testified in court that their involvement was limited to only photos and no physical involvement, but this information helped Mike's defense. His attorneys claimed that Greer's involvement compromised the case against Mike with Nicole.

Still, none of that affected the trial's outcome and the jury returned a guilty verdict. Mike Adams was convicted of capital murder. In Texas, capital murder carries an automatic sentence of life in prison without the possibility of parole.

CHAPTER 11
THE GLAMOUR GIRL SLAYER

From an early age, Harvey Glatman had a strange fascination with rope. At the tender age of three, Harvey's mother caught him with a string tied around his penis. He had placed the opposite end of the string in a drawer, closed the drawer, and leaned back.

As a toddler, Harvey showed more strange behavior. He laughed or cried for no apparent reason and had no interest in playing games or with his toys. Then, at age four, his mother caught him with a rope tied around his neck; the free end was thrown over a pipe. He was pulling on the rope with one hand and pulling on his penis with the other. Where a boy of only four in the 1930s gets these ideas, we will never know.

In 1937, at age ten, his family moved from The Bronx, NY, to Denver, Colorado. The following year, Harvey's parents noticed he had red rope burns around his neck. Harvey had been masturbating while hanging himself with a rope to the point of blackout. Harvey's father ridiculed him for his odd behavior, telling him masturbating would give him acne and make him "queer."

By the time he entered junior high school, Harvey did indeed have acne, a set of very large ears, and buck teeth. The kids at school bullied him for his looks and his extreme fear of girls. He turned bright red if a girl even spoke to him. As a result, schoolmates nicknamed him "weasel" and "chipmunk."

His fascination with ropes, bondage, and autoerotic asphyxiation continued. Harvey's parents took him to a psychiatrist, where he was prescribed medication.

By the time he reached high school, he had begun breaking into women's homes. He only wanted to steal an item, usually a piece of clothing, but anything would do. He just wanted a trophy of some sort to prove that he had power over the women. However, he seemed more fascinated with the thrill of the act rather than the actual trophy.

Eventually, just breaking in wasn't enough. At twelve, he followed a woman home to find out where she lived. Later, he broke into her home, tied her with rope, and gagged her. He then fondled her breasts through her clothes.

Sometimes, he broke into women's houses, tied them up, sat them on the couch, and fondled and cuddled them while he forced them to watch sitcoms with him. He thrived on their fear.

He continued to break into houses to steal items and acquired a .38 revolver at seventeen. He then used the gun to stop random women on the street and threaten them, taking their money and forcing them to remove their clothes. Occasionally, he'd snatch a woman's purse, run a few steps, and then turn around and throw the bag back at her. This, again, was to show his power over them.

In May 1945, Harvey abducted Noreen Laurel, drove her out of town, and groped her breasts but didn't rape her. Instead, he drove her back home, where she immediately contacted the police. Noreen later identified Harvey from police photos, and he was arrested only for attempted burglary.

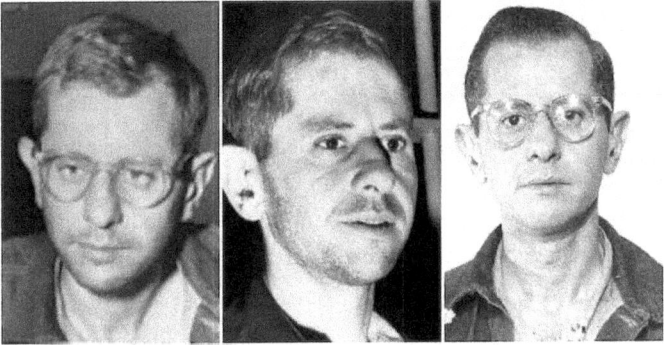

Harvey Glatman

Harvey's mother paid $2,000 to bail him out of jail, but he had molested another woman within a month. This time, he was arrested, convicted, and sent to the Colorado State Prison. Although he was still in high school and in the top percentage of his class, Harvey didn't graduate because he was in jail. After serving only eight months, Harvey Glatman was released for good behavior.

Just three weeks after leaving the Colorado State Prison, Glatman mugged a young couple by pulling a cap gun on them. The weapon was just a toy, but the couple had no idea. He tied the man with a rope and pawed at the woman's breasts. When the man tried to escape, Glatman stabbed him in the shoulder and ran.

Just days later, Glatman fled back east to Albany, New York, and continued his mayhem. He mugged and groped several young, unsuspecting women and was again arrested.

By the time he was twenty-one, Harvey Glatman was serving a ten-year sentence in Sing Sing Correctional Facility, where psychologists diagnosed him with a psychopathic personality and a high IQ.

Again, Glatman was a model prisoner and was released early after serving only three years. Police sent him back to Denver to finish his parole while living with his mother.

Harvey Glatman's parole ended in September 1956, and he was no longer required to live in Denver. He quickly packed up and moved to Los Angeles, California. When he arrived in LA, he worked as a television repairman – a trade he had learned while in prison.

Ever since his high school years, Harvey had held a fascination with photography. Once he was set up in the Los Angeles area, he realized that plenty of beautiful women desperately wanted to be movie stars and models. However, once they realized how hard it was to get into the movies, they quickly turned to posing as pin-up girls. Glatman saw an opportunity and placed an ad in a newspaper looking for models. Before long, beautiful young women were calling him and begging for work.

On August 1, 1957, a nineteen-year-old model named Judy Dull answered his ad. Judy was going through a bitter divorce and was trying to get custody of her child. She was an aspiring actress but was desperate for money to pay for a lawyer and so agreed to meet Glatman for a photo shoot.

Harvey's ad claimed he needed photos for a detective magazine, known in the 1950s as "pulp fiction" magazines. When

Judy arrived wearing a tight skirt and sweater, as he requested, Glatman bound her with ropes and gagged her mouth. She believed it was all part of the photo shoot. He took photos of her and told her to look frightened, just as she would on the cover of a detective magazine. Then he escalated his sadistic game. Glatman pulled a gun on her to get photos of her *truly* looking frightened. He then untied her legs, left her hands bound, and raped her. At thirty years old, it was the first time Harvey Glatman had ever had intercourse. All the while, he documented the event with photos.

After he finished, he told Judy he would release her. He walked her back to his car but had no intention of driving her home. Instead, he drove east on Interstate 10 toward Indio, California, and into the desert. He then threw her on her stomach with her hands and feet still tied. He tied another rope to the binding on her feet, looped it around her neck, put his knee in the small of her back, and pulled. He strangled Judy Dull to death in the middle of the California desert. Glatman then posed her for a few post-mortem photos and buried her body in a shallow grave.

When Judy's roommate couldn't get in touch with her, she tried to call the phone number she had for the photographer, but it had been disconnected. Her roommate had never met the photographer, so the police had nothing to go on and assumed Judy had just left town.

Seven months later, using the alias George Williams, Glatman met a twenty-four-year-old girl through the Patty Sullivan Lonely Hearts Club. On their first date, he picked up Shirley Ann Bridgeford at her home and met several of her relatives. The two planned an evening of dinner and dancing, but the dancing never happened. After dinner, Glatman drove to the Vallecito Mountains and raped her. He then put flashbulbs on his camera to take photos of his victim on the mountainside at night. After the sun rose, he strangled her, posed her, and took photos of her lifeless body.

Glatman's next victim was a twenty-four-year-old model he had again hired for pin-up photos. Ruth Mercado showed up at his apartment only to be tied up and raped. Then, like with Shirley Ann Bridgeford, Glatman took her to the Vallecito Mountains, raped her again, and strangled her to death. Again, he took photos throughout the entire ordeal.

In October 1958, Glatman got the idea of using a legitimate modeling agency. He realized he could get more beautiful top models that way, so he contacted the Diane Studio who assigned him one of their newest models, Lorraine Vigil.

Lorraine had a bad feeling about Glatman from the very beginning. He showed up at 8 p.m. and informed her they were changing the photo shoot location. As they were driving, Lorraine argued with him, but Glatman had had enough of her whining. He pulled the car over to the side of the road and pointed a gun at her. Lorraine, however, wasn't about to let this man have his way with her. She quickly grabbed the gun's barrel and tried to twist it away from him. The gun accidentally fired and grazed her leg, but that didn't stop her. The two continued fighting over the gun and ended up outside the car, on the side of the road. Glatman was a small man, and eventually, Lorraine overpowered him. She yanked the gun from his hands and pistol-whipped him. In an incredible stroke of luck, a police officer saw the scuffle, pulled his car to the side of the road, and arrested Glatman.

During Glatman's interrogation, he confessed to the murders of Judy Dull, Shirley Ann Bridgeford, and Ruth Mercado. After his confession, Glatman led police to the desert to recover the bodies of Ruth Mercado and Shirley Ann Bridgeford.

During the interrogation, Glatman assumed that police had already found a toolbox he had hidden at his house.

> "You know I killed 'em; there's no way you could've known unless you found the toolbox."
>
> "The toolbox?" The detective asked.
>
> "The one in my house with the pictures… the dead girls… that's where I hid them… the pictures… in my toolbox… You know what I mean? You're just playing with me now."

But until that point, the police hadn't known about the toolbox. When they later found the toolbox in his apartment, it was filled with hundreds of photos he had taken and revealed the methodology of his murders. He had a sequence in which he liked to photograph the girls.

He first photographed them looking very innocent, with an excited look on their face, enjoying the photo shoot. In the second series, their faces had a look of horror. They knew they would soon be sexually abused and most likely killed. The final photos were taken after he had strangled the life out of the girls.

Glatman waived his right to a jury trial. Terrified of spending the rest of his life in jail, Glatman wanted the quickest possible route to end his life. He requested the death penalty several times and asked to remove the automatic appeal given to all death penalty cases.

The trial only lasted three days. The prosecution played recordings of Glatman's four-hour interrogation, where he described the murders with great detail and very little emotion. Harvey Glatman was found guilty of two counts of first-degree murder. When the judge handed down the death sentence, Glatman said,

> "It's better this way… I knew this is the way it would be."

Glatman spent the next nine months at San Quentin State Prison awaiting his execution. Coincidentally, the same prison would later hold Charles Manson and Richard Ramirez. Finally, on September 18, 1959, at the age of thirty-one, Glatman went to the gas chamber. The sodium cyanide took twelve minutes to kill him.

In 1966, parts of Glatman's story were used in a movie called Dragnet 1966. They later made the movie into a weekly prime-time TV show. The movie used actual quotes by Glatman:

> "The reason I killed those girls was 'cause they asked me to. They did… all of them… They said they'd rather be dead than be with me."

It is believed that Glatman may have killed other women during his time in Colorado, before he killed Judy Dull. The body of a woman referred to as "Boulder Jane Doe" was discovered in Boulder, Colorado, in 1954, during the same time that Harvey Glatman lived there. She died after being hit by a car. Glatman drove a 1951 Dodge Coronet, and the police believed the damage to her body was consistent with that model of car. Police, however, could never prove it. Fifty-five years later, in 2009, her identity was finally revealed as eighteen-year-old Dorothy Gay Howard from Phoenix, Arizona.

CHAPTER 12

A WALKING SHADOW

L ife in Hawaii in 1929 was much different than today, especially for poor Japanese families. There was a lot of racial tension in Hawaii, mostly between wealthy white people and poor Japanese people. The events in November 1929 would escalate those tensions exponentially.

Myles Fukunaga was the nineteen-year-old eldest son of a Japanese family with seven kids. By all accounts, Myles was a quiet, responsible Japanese boy who stayed out of trouble and worked hard to support his family. However, as the oldest of the large family, much responsibility fell upon Myles.

Myles' father worked long hours, but it wasn't enough for the large family to survive. As a result, Myles had to drop out of high school to work to support the family. He worked eighty-hour weeks at Queen's Hospital, but it still wasn't enough.

The family was several months behind on their rent, and the stress was building in Myles. Twice, he thought he would be better off dead and attempted suicide. He even failed at that task, which added to his humiliation and embarrassment. Myles also suffered from a degenerative dissociative disorder. He had mental issues that were handled differently in those days: they were brushed under the rug.

One morning, there was a knock on the family's front door. When his mother answered the door, Myles could hear her arguing with a representative from the Hawaiian Trust Company. They were there again to collect the back rent, but the family didn't have it. The rent was $35 per month, and when they missed several months' payments, the fees piled on and made the bill unbearable. This fueled the anger inside Myles.

In recent years, Myles had been following two crimes that were in the news. The first was that of Nathan Leopold and Richard Loeb. The two teenage boys had kidnapped and killed a young boy, using a chisel to beat him over the head. They had then sent a ransom letter to his wealthy father. Another kidnapping Myles followed was perpetrated by William Hickman. Hickman had kidnapped a young girl by showing up at her school and posed as an employee of the girl's father. He told the teachers that the girl's father was in a terrible accident; she needed to come with him. Hickman then demanded a ransom from the girl's father and ultimately killed her. Myles thought he could combine these two examples to commit the perfect crime.

Myles called the Punahao School and asked to speak to the registrar. He told the registrar he was calling from Queen's Hospital. He claimed that Gille Jamieson's mother had been in a terrible car accident. They sent a car immediately to pick up the boy.

Using a uniform from the hospital where he worked, Myles posed as a hospital orderly and hired a taxicab to take him to the school of Gille Jamieson, the ten-year-old son of Frederick Jamieson. Frederick Jamieson was Vice President of The Hawaiian Trust Company.

Gille's teacher and the school's principal later told police there was nothing unusual about the young Japanese man who picked up Gilles. Their only description was that he was Japanese, had slicked-back hair, and wore black glasses.

Frederick Jamieson soon received a ransom note from Myles, peppered with strange Shakespeare quotes from Macbeth.

"Life's but a walking shadow, a poor player, that struts and frets his hour upon the stage and then is heard no more."

It seemed that Myles was dramatically referencing his desperation and lack of will to live. The ransom note demanded $10,000 for the safe release of his son.

But Myles had no intention of releasing the young boy. Instead, before the Jamieson family had a chance to respond to the ransom, Myles took Gilles behind the Seaside Hotel – where the International Marketplace now stands on Kalakaua Avenue, just opposite the Royal Hawaiian Hotel – to a grouping of kiawe trees. There, he took a hardened steel chisel, similar to what he had read that Leopold and Loeb used, and beat the boy over the head. He then strangled him to death.

When the media heard about the missing boy, the entire island of Oahu was on alert. Racial tensions flared because the young boy was white, and the kidnapper was said to be Japanese. Japanese businesses had to close because they were getting threats from white people.

Everyone was looking for the boy. The Oahu Schools let out early, and twenty thousand students joined in the search for Gilles across the island. The Jamiesons had a chauffeur they had fired some weeks prior, and he became the first suspect. Harry Kaisan was arrested, brought in for questioning, and put under the influence of a "truth serum." In those days, people believed Hyoscine Hydrobromide would force people to tell the truth. Amazingly, it's still used in some parts of the world today. Kaisan was ultimately found innocent and released.

Frederick Jamieson received a phone call from the kidnapper. The man said to meet him at a band concert on Thomas Square and to bring $4,000, at which point he would give up the boy. No cops. Jamieson did as he was told and didn't tell the police. Myles showed up wearing a black mask, took the money from Jamieson, and disappeared into the crowd without saying a word about the boy.

Jamieson had paid the $4,000 in $5 bills, and as a banker, he had noted the serial numbers. Police alerted local businesses to watch for the bills, and it wasn't long before Myles was caught trying to buy a train ticket with the money. When apprehended, Myles quickly confessed.

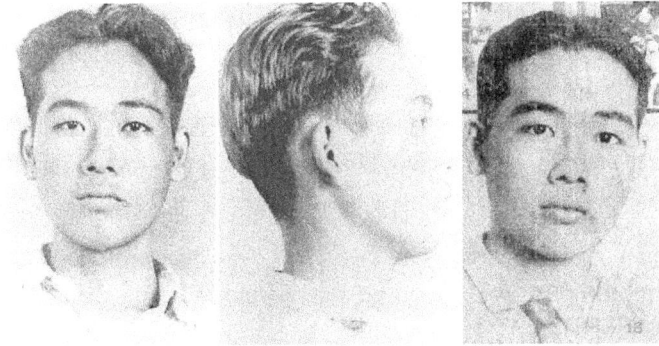

Myles Fukunaga

About the same time that Myles was arrested, the body of Gilles Jamieson was found in Waikiki. Myles had covered his body with newspapers and a piece of cardboard. On the cardboard, Myles wrote:

> "If you want to die, you have the right to kill others so that you, in turn, will be killed. The devil it is for you to decide."

The arrest of Myles Fukunaga ignited outrage throughout the island. Twenty thousand people gathered outside the jail after his arrest. Police called the fire department to deal with the massive mob and sprayed seven streams of water at the crowds to try and disperse them. The angry mob demanded a swift and powerful punishment.

Swift it was. Police couldn't handle the pressure from the public and wanted the whole ordeal over with as quickly as possible; it seemed that Myles wanted the same. As a result, Myles Fukunaga was arrested, tried, convicted, and sentenced to hang in just three weeks.

Fukunaga was examined quickly by three psychiatrists appointed by the police for only ninety minutes. The examinations typically took several days at that time, but the police felt the pressure and needed to rush to a judgment. Psychiatrists determined that he was competent and ready to stand trial. Myles Fukunaga freely admitted his guilt and asked specifically to be hanged. The prosecution was more than happy to oblige.

In a gross violation of his rights, his two court-appointed public defenders offered no defense and called no witnesses. Though he admitted to killing the boy, Fukunaga was not allowed to enter a guilty plea. Instead, they wanted him hanged and forced him to plead not guilty. A Navy psychiatrist offered to enter his testimony for the defense but was denied.

The jury appointed to the case included members of the search party, the man who dug the boy's grave, and even Frederick Jamieson's personal bodyguard. Despite several attempts for an appeal to show that Fukunaga was mentally unable to stand trial, they denied all requests.

The crime and conviction opened large divisions on Oahu between the whites and the Japanese. Japanese families throughout Hawaii felt a sense of fear and resentment for years after the crime. Fukunaga's family was constantly harassed and even moved to Maui to escape ostracization.

Myles Fukunaga was ultimately convicted of first-degree murder and hanged at Oahu Prison on November 19, 1929, just two months after he kidnapped and killed Gilles Jamieson.

The story of the killing is still told as a ghost story every Halloween to this day in Hawaii.

"Until we have understood his personality so thoroughly and the circumstances of his life so fully that we can actually feel how he came to act as he did, we have not given him the defense to which he is morally entitled. We cannot discover to what extent society is to blame for this hideous crime or what social changes we should endeavor to bring about."

- University of Hawaii Professor Dr. Lockwood Myrick in a letter to then-Governor Farrington over ninety years ago.

CHAPTER 13
BONUS CHAPTER: THE BROOMSTICK KILLER

T his chapter is a free bonus chapter from True
Crime Case Histories: Volume 4

———

The tale of The Broomstick Killer is easily one of the most
sinister stories in Texan history. Kenneth McDuff was a
bloodthirsty killer who was granted unprecedented leniency
by a justice system that allowed him to continue killing even
after he had shown that he was a sadistic psychopath.

———

The tiny town of Rosebud in central Texas was the home of a
notoriously strange family: the McDuffs. J.A. McDuff, the
father, owned a cement finishing business that did quite well
during the building boom of the late seventies, and the
family was well-off by small town standards. The mother,
Addie McDuff, ran the laundromat across from their home

and doted over her six children. She was a large, headstrong woman known for being over-protective of her children, and would come running if they ever encountered trouble.

Addie was notoriously known to carry a gun in her purse and was referred to as the "Pistol-Packin' Mama" by the locals in Rosebud. Her children's teachers feared her because she would storm into the school in a huff any time one of her children was accused of misconduct. To Addie, her children could do no wrong whatsoever, and if someone accused them of anything, the school was likely to blame.

The eldest son, Lonnie, was the bully of the family. He once pulled a knife on the school principal who subsequently threw him down a flight of stairs. Lonnie spoke with a speech impediment and referred to himself as "Wuff and Tuff Wonnie McDuff."

Addie McDuff was particularly fond of her youngest son, Kenneth. Though technically he wasn't the youngest of the children, she fawned over him as her "baby boy." Even in his early teens when Kenneth started getting into trouble, somebody else was always to blame in her eyes.

Kenneth was a known troublemaker and a bully like his older brother Lonnie. He was always the kid with a pocketful of money, and new clothes, and he rode a loud motorcycle to school. Though he had an average IQ, he didn't do well in school. Kenneth didn't seem to care about school and his only genuine friend was his brother Lonnie.

By the fall of 1964 Kenneth was seventeen and spent most of his time causing trouble. He broke into businesses and homes looking for things to steal and drove around town looking for girls. But he wasn't looking for a girl to date: He was looking for a girl to rape. McDuff confided in his brother that he had once raped a woman, slit her throat, and left her dying. Whether the story was authentic is uncertain, as the crime was never reported.

Even at an early age, local law enforcement was all too familiar with Kenneth McDuff. Inevitably he was arrested in 1965 for a string of more than a dozen burglaries. The sentence for his crimes totaled fifty-two years, but because he was only eighteen the judge was lenient. McDuff was allowed to serve his time concurrently instead of consecutively. The fifty-two years of prison was reduced to a meager three years, and he only ended up serving ten months before they released him.

The brief sentence gave McDuff a sense of invincibility and just eight months later he moved on to much more heinous crimes.

On a hot August night in 1966, McDuff and his new friend Roy Dale Green were on their way to Fort Worth. Roy assumed they were on their way to drink some beer and look for girls, but McDuff had much more diabolical plans in mind.

Roy Dale Green was a skinny eighteen-year-old who was impressed with, and excited to be hanging out with twenty-year-old McDuff. Green knew that McDuff was a trouble-maker, but when Kenneth told him he wanted to rape a girl that night, Roy didn't take him seriously. When McDuff pulled into the parking lot of the baseball field in Everman, Texas, Roy had no idea what a mess he had got himself into.

McDuff pulled his car up next to a parked car near the baseball diamond; he could see there were three teenagers inside the car. He reached under the seat and pulled out a Colt .38 revolver, got out of the car, and walked up to the driver's side door of the parked car.

Pointing the revolver at the window, McDuff ordered the three teens out of the car. Inside the car was sixteen-year-old Edna Louise Sullivan, her boyfriend seventeen-year-old Robert Brand, and his fifteen-year-old cousin Mark Dunham. McDuff led them to the trunk of the car and commanded them to get in. The three teens climbed in, and he closed the lid.

McDuff drove their car while Roy Green followed in McDuff's car to an isolated area where they stopped. McDuff and Green got out of the cars and McDuff turned to Green and said, "We're gonna have to knock 'em off." Kenneth then opened the trunk and pulled Edna out. The teen girl screamed as he dragged her away from her friends to his own car and locked her in his trunk. He then went back over to the young boys. Unable to see, Edna's terror only intensified when she heard six gunshots. McDuff had emptied the revolver into the two other boys' bodies. When he could not close the trunk, McDuff became frustrated and backed the car up to a fence and abandoned it with the boy's bodies hanging out of the back.

Roy Green was in shock. They both got back in to McDuff's car and drove to another location where McDuff pulled Edna out of the back of the car and raped her. After he raped her, McDuff ordered Green to rape her too. Then McDuff yelled to Green, "Find something for me to strangle her with." Green pulled the belt off of his pants and handed it to him, but McDuff found something he liked better. He had a broom in the back of his car. He raped her with the broomstick, then sat on her chest and held it across her neck. He leaned forward on the broomstick, putting more and more pressure on her neck until he crushed her throat. McDuff threw her body over his shoulder, walked to the side of the dirt road and tossed her body into the nearby bushes; the two drove away.

The next day Roy Green was consumed with guilt and told his friend's mother what they had done. His friend's mother went to Green's mother, who subsequently convinced him to turn himself in.

Green was arrested and led the police to the bodies, and McDuff was quickly arrested as well. Green gave the police the gun that McDuff had buried next to his garage.

During the trial, a terrified Roy Green stuttered and stammered as he testified against McDuff. McDuff was cocky and nonchalant, taking the stand in his own defense, but it didn't help his case.

In November 1966 a jury found Kenneth McDuff guilty on three counts of murder. Roy Green served eleven years in prison for his part in the murders, while McDuff was handed three death sentences in the electric chair. In a normal world, this would be the end of the story, but it was nowhere near over.

On June 29, 1972 after six years on death row, the US Supreme Court decided that the death penalty, as it was then written, was a cruel and unusual punishment and was therefore unconstitutional under the Eighth and Fourteenth Amendments. In an extraordinary event, all death penalty cases in the United States were commuted to life sentences.

McDuff was now eligible for parole and applied for it every time he was allowed. He was convicted of such heinous crimes; it was unimaginable that he would ever be paroled.

The residents of Central Texas thought that such a vicious killer could never be paroled. Over and over he applied, and he was repeatedly denied.

Fifteen years later in 1987, McDuff saw his chance. The Texas Federal Court ruled that the prisons of Texas were far too overcrowded, violating the civil rights of the inmates. Rather than spend money building more prisons, the courts set population limits in the prisons which led to a massive backlog of inmates being held in county jails across the state.

Texas Governor Bill Clements made an unthinkable deal with the parole board. In order to reduce prison population, they were required to release 150 inmates per day. Initially, the white-collar crimes were released, then the minor drug offenses. Within two years the only people left in the prisons were murderers. This is when McDuff saw his chance.

Each time he applied for parole, McDuff still had to appear before a parole board of three members, plead his case, and get two out of three votes in his favor. He had tried several times and was denied each time. In one instance he actually received two votes, but it was ultimately denied when an unknown party argued against his release. In another instance he tried to bribe a parole board official by offering him $10,000. Each time he was denied, but it didn't deter him.

Outside of the prison, McDuff's mother was busy doing her part. She hired two well-known attorneys from Huntsville, paying them $2,200 to try to find a way to get her beloved son released from prison.

Unbelievably, in 1989, after serving twenty-three years in prison, McDuff was paroled. The two members of the parole board that voted to release him were James Granberry and

Chris Mealy. Mealy later blamed the tremendous pressure he was under from the government. Granberry was later charged with perjury in an unrelated case and ordered to serve six months in a halfway house.

During those years, the Texas parole board set free 127 murderers and twenty death row inmates.

———

The people of Rosebud were in shock at the news of McDuff's release. Some put bars over their windows and many feared walking the streets of the tiny town without a gun.

Immediately after his release, McDuff was required to visit his parole officer in Temple, Texas. After their first visit, the parole officer told police,

> "I don't know if it'll be next week or next month or next year, but one of these days, dead girls are gonna start turning up, and when that happens, the man you need to look for is Kenneth McDuff."

The parole officer was right. Just three days after his release, the body of twenty-nine-year-old Sarafia Parker was found in a field twenty-five miles west of Rosebud in Temple, the town that McDuff's parents had moved to while he was in prison. Though they had no evidence, police suspected McDuff was responsible for the killing.

McDuff was known as a racist. Just seven months after his release he harassed a young black man in Rosebud, yelling racial slurs at him, and pulled a knife on him. This violated his parole, and he was quickly sent back to prison, but

McDuff knew how the prison system worked. He knew about the overcrowding issues and he was back on the streets just two months later.

After his release from prison, McDuff enrolled at Texas State Technical College in Waco and briefly got a job as a cashier at a convenience store called Quik-Pak. But working for a lowly $4 an hour did not satisfy him, and he quit after only a month.

By the summer of 1991, McDuff had given up his feeble attempts at the straight-and-narrow life and continued his life of crime. Living in the college dorms, he started dealing and using drugs. He knew this violated his parole, but he didn't care. He spent his spare time picking up prostitutes in Waco and used them to satisfy his need for violent sex.

In the late hours of October 10, 1991, McDuff picked up a young crack-addicted prostitute from Waco, Brenda Thompson, intent on killing her. McDuff had Brenda tied up in the passenger seat of his red pickup truck when he noticed a police checkpoint up ahead. Brenda saw her opportunity and screamed as she raised her legs up to the windshield and began kicking, cracking the windshield several times. When the police ran toward his truck McDuff hit the gas and crashed the roadblock. Several police officers had to jump out of the way to avoid being run over.

McDuff led police on a high-speed chase but escaped into the night by turning off his lights and driving the wrong way down one-way streets. After he escaped, he took Brenda Thompson down an old abandoned road into a wooded area near Route 84 where he raped, tortured, and murdered her. Her body wasn't found until seven years later.

Just a week later McDuff picked up another Waco prostitute. Seventeen-year-old Regina DeAnne Moore was last seen arguing outside a motel with McDuff on the night of October 17. Again, McDuff tied her arms and legs with her own stockings, then took her to a remote area where he raped and murdered her. Her remains were not found until 1998.

Two months later in Austin, twenty-eight-year-old Colleen Reed was washing her shiny new Mazda Miata convertible at a self-serve car wash.

One thing that McDuff learned in prison was to find a malleable sidekick. That evening he was driving around Austin with his latest sidekick, Alva Hank Worley. As they drove past the car wash McDuff spotted Colleen and made a quick U-turn.

McDuff pulled his tan Thunderbird into the bay next to hers, got out of the car and walked into Colleen's stall. Without a word, McDuff grabbed her around the neck and lifted the tiny girl off the ground. When Colleen screamed, neighbors behind the car wash came out to see what was happening. They watched as McDuff threw Colleen in his car and he and Worley drove away, again driving the wrong way on a one-way street.

The witnesses got a good look at Worley and alerted the police of his description and the type and color of the vehicle that sped away. Right away police suspected that McDuff was behind the abduction.

When police got the description of Worley, they began looking through McDuff's known associates and noticed Hank Worley immediately as one of his known drinking buddies. Like Roy Dale Green, Worley was timid and easily influenced by McDuff.

Worley wasn't hard to find, living in a motel with his four-teen-year-old daughter. When police knocked on his door, he was already terrified with guilt.

Though his guilt consumed him, he feared McDuff and wasn't quite ready to point a finger at him. On the first visit to his motel room, Worley claimed he barely knew McDuff. It took a few visits to his motel room for police to persuade him to admit to what had happened that night. They stopped by while he was having a barbecue by the motel pool with his daughter, and Detective Mike McNamara whispered in his ear,

> "Hank, you're hiding a kid killer, you know that? You're protecting a man who raped and brutalized and strangled a girl not much older than your daughter over there. Picture her on the ground, a broomstick across her throat, crying out for you to help, begging you to speak out, to do what's right, to save the life of some young girl, to…"

McNamara couldn't finish his sentence before Worley screamed. He was ready to talk. When investigators got him into the interrogation room, he told the complete story of the night of Colleen's abduction.

Worley said he and McDuff were in Austin looking for drugs when McDuff saw Colleen washing her car. When McDuff lifted her off the ground by her throat she screamed "Please, not me! Not me!" He then threw her in the back of their car and told Worley to hold her down as they sped off.

When they got a few miles out of Austin McDuff got in the back with Colleen and commanded Worley to keep driving out of town. McDuff tied her hands behind her back with her shoelaces, then took his cigarette and put it out between her legs as she screamed. He beat her and raped her. When he finished, he told Worley to change places with him and Worley raped her while McDuff drove.

> Worley recalled, "I didn't want to have sex with her but if I didn't have sex with her, I knew that he was gonna get back there with her and beat her up some more and burn her with cigarettes. He was taking the cigarettes and getting the fire real hot and burning her down there in the wrong spots."

When they got near the town of Belton, McDuff pulled onto a secluded dirt road and raped her again.

> "He turned around, and he hit her. Slapped her real hard and knocked her backwards. Then he took another cigarette, and he lit it, and got the fire real hot and he burned her like that again."

When she was able to stand Worley claimed Colleen put her head on his shoulder and said "Please don't let him hurt me anymore." McDuff was having none of that. He grabbed her by the neck and stuffed her into the trunk of the car and turned to Worley and said, "I'm gonna use her up." McDuff used the term often to mean that he was going to terminate her life.

> "Then he put her in the trunk of the car, closed the trunk down and he takes me home. On the way home he asked me for my pocketknife and I told him I don't know where it is."
>
> "Then he asked me, 'Well, I need a shovel. Let me borrow a shovel.' And I said, 'I ain't got one.' He didn't say what he was

going to do with it, but I knew what he was gonna do with it. He wanted to kill her with it."

"Ain't nothin' I could do. Real scary being like that. If you can't help yourself, there ain't no way you gonna help anybody else. I wasn't even sure if I was gonna make it outta that."

"I'll always have a tear for that girl. I'll always cry for her, for what she went through. Nobody should be put through that type of torture."

McDuff was nowhere to be found, but police knew he was still in the area the following February when they found the body of another young prostitute. Twenty-two-year-old Valencia Joshua, a student at the same college that McDuff had attended was found on a golf course near the school. She had been strangled. The last time anyone had seen her, she was looking for Kenneth McDuff on the campus of their school.

Then on March 1, 1992, Melissa Northrup was working the night-shift at the Quik-Pak convenience store. She was a pregnant mother of two who knew the dangers of working the night shift, but needed to pay the bills. She would regularly call her husband during her shift to let him know she was okay.

Late that night McDuff was cruising the streets looking for drugs when his tan Thunderbird broke down just 100 yards from the Quik-Pak. This was the same store that McDuff had worked for only a month. McDuff knew that the store was open twenty-four hours a day and had no security to speak of. He also knew that there was a cute twenty-three-year-old who worked the night shift and had told friends that the place could easily be robbed.

When Melissa's husband didn't hear from her at 4:00 a.m. that night he got worried and called the store. He repeatedly got no answer so he drove to the store, but there was no sign of his wife.

When police found McDuff's car abandoned at the New Road Inn just 100 yards away, their suspicions were confirmed. McDuff was on a killing spree, and they started a massive nationwide manhunt.

Knowing how close McDuff was with his family, they started by questioning his parents. As always, his mother stood by her beloved son and claimed he was innocent but didn't know where he was. His father, however, was less loving,

> "I don't know where he is. If you find him, you can kill him if you want to."

On April 26, the badly decomposed body of Quik-Pak employee Melissa Northrup was found floating in a gravel quarry in Dallas County. Her hands were still tied behind her back with shoelaces - a signature of Kenneth McDuff.

The big break came on May 1 when the manhunt was aired on America's Most Wanted. The TV show was massively popular; through the years it has helped capture 1,200 fugitives. This airing was no exception. Shortly after it aired a man called from Kansas City, Missouri claiming that McDuff worked for a trash company under the assumed name Richard Fowler.

Texas police called Kansas City police who looked up the name Richard Fowler in their records. Someone had been using the name and had been arrested and fingerprinted for soliciting prostitutes. The fingerprints matched that of

Kenneth McDuff. McDuff was arrested on May 4, 1992 as he was driving a trash truck to a landfill.

When he was brought back to Texas, crowds of angry people gathered outside of the courthouse. McDuff embraced the media and professed his innocence to the mob of cameras outside, often claiming that his trial was unfair.

Prosecutors had their strongest evidence against him for the abduction and murder of Melissa Northrup, so they decided to try that case first and worry about the rest later.

Addie McDuff, who was now seventy-seven years old, was called as a hostile witness to testify against her son. She confirmed that her son used her credit card near the Quik-Pak store on the night of the abduction, putting him near the scene of the crime when it happened.

McDuff was livid that his own mother was being used by the prosecution to testify against him, but there was more to come. The prosecution called two of his friends to testify that he had tried to enlist them in his plans to rob the Quik-Pak store.

At one point McDuff directed his anger at his own attorneys when he screamed at them,

> "Why don't you get up and go sit on the prosecution's side! You're helping them more than you are me!"

The murder of Colleen Reed had not been tried yet, and the prosecution called Hank Worley to testify to show that there was a signature to McDuff's killings. Worley was brought to the courthouse in handcuffs. From his visible shaking, it was clear that just being in the presence of McDuff again terrified him.

The ultimate nail in the coffin for McDuff was when he insisted on testifying on his own behalf despite his defense team's wishes. They explained to him that under the rules of evidence, his past 1966 murders couldn't be mentioned in court if he wasn't on the stand, but if he took the stand, the prosecution could use that against him. McDuff wouldn't listen.

McDuff took the stand for two hours rambling a nonsensical story of his whereabouts on the night of the murder. Meanwhile, the prosecution took advantage of their opportunity and the jury heard the complete story of his brutal killings of the teenagers in 1966.

The jury took four hours to return their guilty verdict on February 16, 1993. His defense team requested leniency and asked for a life sentence, but the jury only took one hour to decide that Kenneth McDuff should die by lethal injection.

McDuff's trial for the murder of Colleen Reed started in 1994. Although the body had still not been found, he was given a second death sentence.

In television interviews from prison awaiting his death sentence, McDuff continued to profess his innocence, even for the 1966 killings.

In the months before his execution, investigators enlisted the help of a jailhouse informant to try to get McDuff to give up the locations of the bodies. Their plan worked.

In September 1998, the body of Regina DeAnne Moore was found beneath a bridge on the side of a highway. McDuff had buried her in a shallow grave. Her hands were still tied behind her back with shoelaces, and her ankles were bound with stockings.

The body of Brenda Thompson, who kicked McDuff's wind-shield as he crashed through the roadblock, was found in a grouping of trees outside of Waco. She had been tied up, raped, and tortured.

McDuff only had two weeks before his execution, but he wasn't giving up the location of Colleen Reed. He told the informant that he didn't want to tell the cops because it was the last body and if he gave them everything they needed they would "take away my commissary rights, and won't treat me right." With only two weeks to live, McDuff's only concern was his own diminished rights and had no regard for the closure of his victim's families.

Police met with prison officials and arranged to take none of his prison rights away. Presented with the assurance, McDuff finally gave them directions to where he had buried Colleen Reed's body.

Despite digging for hours exactly where he told them, they were unable to locate her body. That afternoon, in a covert arrangement, McDuff was brought to the dig site. The body of Colleen Reed was found on October 6, 1998.

In McDuff's final days investigator John Moriarty spent over forty hours interviewing him, trying to gain a deeper under-standing of the psychopath's mind. In the time he spent with him, though he showed no remorse at all, McDuff admitted to all eight murders and alluded that there may have been many more.

Kenneth McDuff was executed on November 17, 1998. His family didn't claim his body, and he was buried in in the Huntsville prison graveyard with a tombstone that displayed only his death row number X999055 and the day of execution.

As a result of the mayhem that McDuff caused and an outcry from the public, the Texas parole system was completely overhauled and the state spent $2 billion building more prisons.

———

This chapter is a free bonus chapter from True Crime Case Histories: Volume 4

CHAPTER 14
APPENDIX A: "SK CONFESSIONS" BY MARK TWITCHELL

T he text that follows is the document *"SK Confessions"* that was found by detectives on Mark Twitchell's computer and used as evidence against him. He had deleted the file, but forensic investigators were able to recover it. Twitchell goes into excruciating detail about his assault of Johnny Altinger and the dismemberment and disposal of his body. It's a jarring look inside the mind of the psychopathic killer.

———

This story is based on true events. The names and events were altered slightly to protect the guilty.

This is the story of my progression into becoming a serial killer. Like anyone just starting out in a new skill, I had a bit of trial and error in the beginning of my misadventures. Allow me to start from the beginning and I think you'll see what I mean.

I don't remember the exact place and time it was that I decided to become a serial killer but I remember the sensation that hit me when I committed to the decision. It was a rush of pure euphoria. I felt lighter, less stressed if you will at the freedom of the prospect. There was something about urgently exploring my dark side that greatly appealed to me and I'm such a methodical planner and thinker, the very challenge itself was enticing to behold.

This realization was just the last in a series of new discoveries I made about myself.

I just knew I was different somehow from the rest of humanity. I feel no such emotions as empathy or sympathy toward others for example.

Of course when it came to actual one on one conversations with therapists, I had to lie. I mean talk about leaving a trail of bread crumbs. The last thing I needed to do was air out all of my darkest fantasies and half formed plans to someone who is legally obligated to contact the authorities if they think a patient will do harm to themselves or others. I'm not stupid. Nevertheless, deception aside, it was a useful exercise to get to know my label better.

When a man approaches thirty years of age, he tends to question what his ultimate purpose is in this world and where he fits into the picture. And then I remembered something else. A passage I read from a novel by the renowned fantasy writer, David Gemmell in reference to a bronze age assassin. I can't recall the exact wording but it was the philosophy that hit home. The assassin reflected on what he does with his life with guilt (another emotion I am incapable of) and someone imparted a bigger picture wisdom.

He said that the assassin is the hand of fate. Fate has already decided everyone's time to die from the moment they are born. When it's their time, it's their time and if they do not die of old age or sickness, when their time comes other factors are employed by fate to get the job done. I think about that whenever I plan a kill. It's not me who chooses the victims but fate. Oh sure I choose the victim to match my own criteria in the interest of remaining free and at large, but for the most part I am merely following my own nature which was devised by the grand design of the universe.

Now this does not mean I shirk responsibility for my actions. I am very obviously, as you will come to learn, deliberate, level headed and very much in control of my own actions. Although I won't deny that the aforementioned scenario would play well in an insanity plea.

So here I was, armed with this new insight into my inner self and an exhilarating new hobby that I was seeking to undertake. I thought long and hard to come up with a system that would work for me, a method that would ensure I could have my play time and keep from getting caught. It didn't take long before I settled on an M.O.

I would use online dating to rope in my victims. Once I came up with that one clear starting point, all of the other pieces needed to be tended to. I began to ask myself a series of questions designed to get me to consider every possible angle. I wanted to have every step in the process already planned out from start to finish because improvising would be bad and lead to sloppiness. I had to have an order, a plan, something that would bring calm to a chaotic situation.

First question: Who do I want to target? At first I considered married men looking to cheat on their wives. In one way I'd be taking out the trash, doling out justice to those who on some level, deserved what they got. But the logic of the situation denies this possibility. After all people who are expected home at a certain hour tend to get reported as missing and there's other factors that would lead to an investigation I didn't want. No, I had to choose people whose entire lives I could infiltrate and eliminate evidence of my existence from on all levels.

I finally settled on middle-aged single men who lived alone. My reasons were numerous. For one thing, they would be easy to lead by their dicks, easy to manipulate, easy to seduce under my fake female disguises. They were also the most likely targets to have the most expendable money in their bank accounts. A tidbit I would use to my advantage later on. Finally, by living alone, once they were out of the picture I could easily enter their living spaces undetected with no forced entry and remove all sorts of valuable items from the premises.

Oh yes my friend, I am in this for profit. It has always been my attitude that no hobby or venture should ever be done without expected return on investment. For many years I crafted elaborate Halloween costumes, faithful screen accurate recreations of very big blockbuster movie icons. The result of my efforts in these costumes, were various 1st prizes in costume contests that resulted in cash payouts worth at least forty times what I spent to make each outfit. This would be no different.

I had expenses with this new hobby and I would make sure that I generated a profit from it to recoup and eclipse my costs. That was the next step in the process for being fully prepared, a detailed shopping list of all the items I would need to carry out my plans.

First off I needed a location. I scoured listings to find something suitable. I started looking in regular secure storage but the video surveillance and inability to get my victims there smoothly threw that idea out the window quickly. When I finally found my location it could not have been any more perfect.

A double detached garage for rent in the south of the city, tucked away in a quiet neighborhood on a lot with a house occupied by tenants who couldn't even read English, much less speak it, no doubt work program immigrants brought in by a donut chain with supplied housing.

Everything, I decided, would take place here. The approach, the apprehension and the kill as well as preparation for disposal of the body could all be done in relative seclusion from this one building. Total privacy. I immediately went to work removing the address plank from the back, blocking out all the windows with boards and duct tape, replacing locks.

The back driveway wasn't even paved, it was just a bed of gravel with grass growing out of it. The entire surrounding area was blocked out of sight from neighbors with high thick fences and the entire block was dead starting at eight o'clock at night.

My shopping list was very thorough. I went out to several different stores to avoid buying all of my items from one location and I paid cash to avoid a paper trail just in case. A street hockey mask, that I would soon cut the mouth out of and paint gold streaks into for dramatic effect. A basic dark green hoody, something comfortable with pockets that hides distinctive marks, body type and hair. Two sets of disposable overalls for what was sure to be a messy clean up process and

I would use the plastic bags all this came in to wrap my shoes for the process.

I bought a hunters game processing kit, which if you think about it is ideal for this scenario. Why not use a whole set of tools designed to take apart large mammals in the forest on the fly? It reduces the spatter caused by power tools, takes the noise level way down too and there's also just something more gratifying about sawing through tendons and bone with your bare hands than using something else that takes the fun out of the work.

My kill knife was different though. I wanted the weapon used for the deed itself to be simple, elegant and beautiful in it's own way so I dropped by a military surplus store and picked up a well crafted hunting knife with an 8 inch blade. I would use this weapon to cleanly and simply slice open a gash in the victims neck allowing them to bleed out quickly and with no pain. I'm not a torture guy. Again, the noise level from the screams is not my thing at all and I only resort to that if they are still alive after apprehension but won't give me the simple information I ask for.

Several rolls of painters plastic sheeting to prep my kill room. At least 6 rolls of packing tape and just as many rolls of duct tape as well as two boxes of contractor grade hefty bags. I picked up a stun baton because I thought that would render my targets without use of their muscles quickly and painlessly and I bought an extra realistic airsoft pistol; something that could very easily be mistaken for the real thing, especially in low light just for that extra edge.

I made sure to acquire construction materials for my custom furniture. I went to town designing and building a rather sturdy four foot by six foot six inch table with stainless steel finish and angle iron edging. I also welded a rather mean looking chair and another table was left there by the realty company, which I used to stay organized on.

Finally I ordered a forty five gallon steel drum which would be the final resting place for the body parts before I incinerated them. I was all set, prepared as I could be. I diligently set up my kill room, creating the plastic bubble I needed to create my nasty mayhem. The trap was set, and now it was time to bait the hook.

I downloaded an IP address blocker first and foremost. I mean it would be rather silly of me to run this whole operation from my home computer without it, just so that if any of my play mates disappearances were ever actually investigated, there would be this electronic trail leading the police directly back to me and my little workshop of horrors.

Once activated, I created all new email addresses and dating site profiles for my dark plan. It was so easy it was almost insulting. But really, who thinks to look outside their pond when they go out fishing? No one. I did a quick search for females that matched what I wanted to represent in other cities around the world and when I found someone I liked, I copied their photos and used them in my new online identity as whoever it was I wanted to be.

I always change things up. I never use the same profile for more than one victim at a time, and I generate new email addresses as well, just in case. After a victim is removed from the world neatly and cleanly, I erase my accounts and every trace they left behind. Sure the mother servers may or may not have an imprinted image, but even if they checked, they wouldn't trace me.

As soon as the profiles go up, within twenty four hours the responses come in like a flood. I review the messages sent and choose my victims based on age, body type, profession, status and living situation. Obviously I'm not going to pursue a 6'4 athletic martial arts instructor who's married with 4 kids. That's just got trouble written all over it. I mean I'm ruthless but I'm not an idiot. I have my own fight training background but I don't have delusions of grandeur.

When I come across a single man in his late thirties to early forties who is self employed, lives alone and stands between 5' 7 and 5' 11 with an average body type weighing in between 150 and 180 lbs, I know I've found my ideal target.

Such was the case with a man I will refer to as Frank. That of course is not his real name and I won't divulge any other sensitive details about the situation but Frank was my very first target ever. I roped him in with a profile I was quite proud of featuring photos of a blonde I would like to bang myself.

I asked him to pick me up from my residence at a prescribed time on a particular night of the week and then gave him detailed instructions on how to find the place. I gave him some song and dance routine about how my landlord had the property setup to where the back gate was broken and padlocked and there was nowhere in front to park because of a no parking zone and a bus stop across the street. So I told him I would leave the garage door open for him to come in through and then to come the back door of the house, all the while realizing of course that he would never make it that far.

So the message was received and confirmed, and I waited.

Generally I was quite pleased with myself. I had a perfectly formulated plan, and I was fully prepared. I adorned my specialty mask, serving the double purpose of facial protection and identity shield to give the victim a false sense of security in thinking they would be let go since I cared about hiding who I was. But without explaining it to them, that thought would not likely cross their mind in the heat of the moment.

I slipped my hoody on and pulled the hood over my head, resting it comfortably over my brow. I slipped the knife holster with the blade in it onto my belt and pulled on my fine leather gloves.

My kill room was perfectly prepped. Plastic sheeting taped together and around my table; a large green cloth screwed into the drywall ceiling to shield view of it from my guests line of sight, and to shield me too of course. I now stood but a few feet away from the front door which I had locked of course. The plan was to wait in the shadow of my curtain until he approached the door and shock him with the stun baton followed by a sleeper hold that would sap away his consciousness so that I could tape him up and set him on my table.

The last thought that crossed my mind before Frank pulled up into the driveway had nothing to do with the event itself, but rather was a mental note that I would need to remember to get a stock of paper towels for miscellaneous clean up in the future.

The cars engine rumbled and its headlights shone bright in the lowering dusk. I thought if his headlights were on a delay self shut off like mine that he would see more than I wanted him to which still wasn't much. Just a few crates of tools and paint cans, normal garage accessories in my opinion. But his headlights turned off as his engine petered out. I heard the sound of the car door opening and closing and then the footsteps that followed.

My head was rushed with adrenaline, my stomach had a half second flutter of butterflies before my resolve strengthened and I stood there, ominous in the dark prepared to strike with my stun baton fully extended and the safety off.

The typical taser guns used by police carry a charge of 50,000 volts and we've seen what they do to the people hit with them. The stun baton boasts 800,000 volts which sounds practically lethal but you have to understand that it isn't the voltage but the amps delivered by the weapon that matter. Either way I was confident in the weapons strength.

My confidence was misplaced.

I took two swift silent steps toward my target and pressing the baton across the back of his neck, pulled the trigger. It shocked and jumped but did little more than merely alert the bastard to what was really going on. It did not render his muscles unusable and the little shit fought back.

I had a distinct advantage. I was taller and outclassed him in tenacity and strength. This was also my environment and he wasn't expecting to run into a psycho in a mask, only a beautiful woman he hoped he would get lucky with. The confusion played to my benefit and I struck him repeatedly. He yelled "what the fuck" at the top of his lungs. The noise was something I had hoped to avoid but I paid it no mind and continued attempting to subdue this defiant little shit.

I dropped the baton and punched him several times in the side of the head but still he would not go down. He broke free and I could tell he would make for the door, for the way he came in so I reached into my pocket and withdrew the gun.

I pointed it straight at him and all of a sudden he took me seriously, his eyes wide. I commanded him to get down on the floor, to which he obeyed quickly. If he lifted his head even the slightest bit I warned him against it. I removed my gloves and went for the duct tape. I tore a piece off and slipped it over his eyes.

It was then that I told him that if he did what I told him to, that I would let him live. I brought one arm down around his back and was reaching for the other arm when he began defying me again.

"No, I can't, I can't do this." He began. Retrospect is of course 20/20 and had I been able to go back to that moment there would have been a hundred things I would have done differently. Obviously overestimating the stun baton is a mistake I would not repeat. The other one was putting up with his bullshit. I should have just pounded him in the back of the head while he was down until he lay unconscious on the floor. I should have shut the big door when I had the chance but everything moved too quickly and I didn't want to take my eyes off him for one second.

He got back to his feet having removed the duct tape and when I pointed the gun at him again, he grabbed it. He gripped down hard, twice and I think I might have seen a gleam in him that indicated he felt the guns construction and realized it was not real but I can't be sure. I still held on for dear life, not willing to give him a blunt object to hit me back with.

Frank made a few feeble attempts to hit me and tried one impotent kick aimed at my groin that I easily deflected. I delivered a head butt to his face and he broke free again. I clutched onto his jacket but he shook himself loose of it and took off for the opening in the door.

He made it into the driveway and that's when I knew I was pooched. I followed him out, not caring anymore who might see me. He was fumbling on the ground. I grabbed him by the leg as if to drag him back into the garage caveman style but my energy was depleting and the human survival instinct is one of the most powerful forces on Earth. He tried to grab at my mask and came quite close to pulling it off. I broke the grasp and he spun away into the alley and sure enough, a couple on an evening stroll saw me coming after him sporting a deer in the headlight look that can only be described as a total lack of comprehension. I stared back at them through my mask for half a moment and then headed back for the cover of my lair.

I don't know why I played it as cool as I did. Maybe it was something Frank said during the skirmish about swearing not to tell anyone if I let him go. Maybe it was my own instincts about reading people and the fear in his eyes that told me deep down, he wouldn't report the incident, but I felt ok.

I still packed any gear up of my own and his stray jacket into a bag. Whatever I felt like keeping I cleaned prints off of and tossed the rest in a dumpster. As a final touch I sent one last warning email to Frank through the dating site telling him I had traced his IP address through his messages and that if he did report me, I would hunt him down where he lives when he least expects it and finish what I started. I threw in a line about having cased the garage, that it wasn't even mine and that I never use the same location twice. My last lie was to tell him he was lucky number eighteen on my spree.

I wasn't sure if I should believe it worked. I walked calmly out to my car, got in and drove away, across the entire city back to my home where my wife and child waited for me.

During the entire trip I kept thinking surely this douche bag would call the police. Not that it mattered if he did. I covered my tracks well.

You see in my day life I'm an independent film-maker and everything in that garage could be easily explained away as props for filming a psychological thriller. How I could be on one side of the city scrapping with a potential kill up until 7:20 pm and be home less than an hour later would have been a stretch at best.

Still, I couldn't shake the foreboding feeling. I kept thinking any moment I'd see flashing lights behind me asking me to pull over, despite my perfect adherence to posted speed limits and cautious observance of the safety belt law. Surely the arresting officer would wonder why I was so sweaty and why there was a bag with a hoody, a jacket, a prohibited stun weapon and a set of handcuffs in my trunk.

But those lights never showed up in my rear view mirror.

I checked my voicemail messages and had two; very unusual this time of night. One from my wife wondering if I could be home by 8:30 so that she could pick up a package before 9:00 and one from my prop guy asking if he could borrow my airsoft pistol. Paranoia set in. My wife wouldn't care about picking up a package this late, she'd wait until tomorrow. Could the cops have gotten to her and convinced her to pretend to get me home quicker so they could arrest me?

But I had to stop and think clearly. This was all happening way too fast. There's no way that was possible, this wasn't a movie, this was real life. Even if the police were contacted, their response time to the location would be in the neighborhood of twenty minutes to two hours and there'd be no way for them to verify who rented the garage that quickly.

My fear subsided and I drove home. I practiced my entire behavior pattern should I come home to police cruisers parked along my front yard. I would rush the door in a panic and upon entering or being stopped by patrolmen I would appear utterly surprised and beg them to know if anything had happened to my precious wife and/or daughter. My genuine shock of their presence would start me on the innocent path in their eyes, and then my cover story of being at a therapy appointment would become my short term alibi until I could confess to the cops later that therapy was a cover story I gave my wife so I could have just one night a week to myself.

Between that and the total lack of hard evidence I'd be free regardless and yet still the nervousness set in.

It's pretty fucking hard to concentrate on anything when you live in constant expectation of the police arriving at your doorstep. It turns out my wife did need to pick up a package, a pilates chair that she wanted me to assemble. The directions couldn't be any more complicated than the directions for making mac and cheese but I had a really hard time because the apprehension was always there.

Every time I heard a car drive by I'd feel compelled to look out the window. I heard a massive group of sirens get closer, and closer and closer. My heart leaped into my chest until I realized there was a house fire somewhere close to the area.

Seeing a police cruiser slowly and deliberately pull around my block was the worst part. But then I remembered our across the street neighbor had an itchy trigger finger for calling the cops when the rowdy teenagers next door partied too loudly and it subsided.

A day passed. I spent that day with my 8 month old daughter as my wife ran errands and kept appointments. Then the day turned to night and once again I was suspicious but nothing happened. That was the night I was totally convinced I had gotten off on this one pretty much scot free.

No patrol car would come to take me away bound in handcuffs to be brought up on assault charges, forever ending my serial killing career before it began and bringing down my marriage with it when my wife finds out what I really am.

That first time experience was the basis for my revised method of operandi.

Previously I wanted my victims alive and conscious after I had subdued them. I wanted to get information from them like their email and dating site passwords as well as the pin codes to their debit cards and credit cards. But this priority is now a distant second to making sure I don't get caught. I got lucky that first time and I wasn't going to assume that would ever happen again if anyone else got loose.

So I had to revise my apprehension system in order for it to go more smoothly. I decided to ramp up the savagery of my attack, leaving no margin for error in rendering a target unconscious within the first ten seconds. I dropped the stun baton for the favor of two 24 inch lengths of galvanized steel piping. I was confident that swinging for the fences to the back of the head would do the trick. I would go on a shopping trip the next day to make it happen.

———

Chapter break

Oh my sweet Laci. Just in case you are wondering, Laci is not my wife, or my daughter. Laci is my ex girlfriend. On paper she's the complete opposite of everything that should be my perfect match. She has two small dogs that she treats like human children and those people usually drive me up the wall.

She's also periodically depressed and suffers from frequent anxiety attacks whereas I usually prefer a much more together woman. All these things exist but I love her uncontrollably and always will.

Laci and I met in my first year of college. I was 19 at the time and unbeknownst to me at the time she was 24. I've always been into older women. The first time I met her I was waiting outside the door of an English class I didn't need to take since the school had just dropped the required grade for my program the night before. Still, I thought it couldn't hurt to ride the class out since I had already paid for it and would possibly use the higher mark for something else in the future.

I sat on the floor writing a story. Laci sat down across from me and simply said "Hi." I said hi back and that was the beginning of the end for us.

Our relationship is always and forever on unstable ground. When we first met she was just trying to be friendly but she had a boyfriend. A very stiff, unemotional, dependable long term boyfriend. I was too young and naive to know where this was headed.

I lied to her from the onset. I lied to her about my heritage and my age. Stupid basic life things that are completely pointless to lie about but I did it anyway. Part of me was insecure about just being myself but part of me also didn't think this relationship would go anywhere since she was taken.

I was wrong. It went somewhere very quickly. We became fast friends, she wanted to be in the story I was writing. We began hanging out on a regular basis. I had lied to her about having a girlfriend myself so as not to appear single and therefore, pathetic. So it was really rather easy for me to show up to class one day pretending to be distraught over my girlfriend having dumped me. That day our friendship grew into something stronger.

We spent more time together, very often curling up on a couch as just friends, while we watched TV and nuzzled. Friends rubbed their faces together affectionately didn't they? These ones did, at least until one night when we couldn't take it anymore and made out like a couple of teenagers, which technically speaking I still was.

It was a long hard complicated battle over the next several months as she hummed and hawed over what to do. She was a serial dater to my future serial killer and had never taken down time between relationships, always afraid to be alone. Eventually she did in fact dump her boyfriend for me but the fast transition left damage. She would act out in inappropriate ways, kiss another guy and then say she had to in order to see if what we had was real.

It was no worse than what I had done to her of course. Toward the end of our relationship she also began to find religion and I knew the end was nigh. It's not that I have a problem with religious people per se, I have some very good friends who are quite religious. It's just that I could see major issues down the line with butting heads over what to teach our kids or how to live our lives. Not to mention the fact that killing people isn't exactly welcomed in the kingdom of the man made, 'make me feel better about myself through guilt' system of the faithful.

I didn't need to wait for any of these issues to wreck our relationship. Eventually one lie after another began to unravel. First at my birthday party when my age was revealed to be a year younger than I told her, and then the death blow when she flat out asked my parents about the family origins in the car one day.

Dishonesty had taken its toll and Laci decided to end the relationship. I was absolutely devastated. Crushed beyond all reckoning. I lost my soul mate, the one true love of my life and would never get over it. I told her as I left that night that I love her more than anyone I've ever loved, that I will never love anyone the same way again and that no one she ever meets will love her with the same intensity, passion and commitment that I do.

Laci tried to tell me I cared for women too much and that I would find someone else. It was remarkable how right I was and how wrong she was about the entire situation.

For eight years I thought about her constantly. Several times I tried to touch base with her to see how she was doing. At one point I made brief contact after I found her in a hotmail member search but she cut things off sharply and quickly, said she was getting engaged and that was it.

I would soon come to find out she hadn't written those responses, but her friend did on her behalf and two weeks later, Laci had changed her mind and wanted to get together but she never reconnected with me.

I went through one failed marriage in the meantime, and so did she. When Laci and I reconnected through a social networking

website, she was just in the process of getting divorced, ironi-
cally from a total sociopath who drained her of all her self
worth. Years of neglect and mistreatment at the hands of a
negative, unaffectionate douchebag who would rather play a
video game than be intimate with her had taken its toll.

By the time I found her again, Laci had forgotten what it had
been like to be in a caring loving relationship. Her self
esteem had been torn to shreds and she had turn to the
unconditional love of her animals to keep her going.

By this time I was already married for the second time, to a
wonderful woman. Tess was everything I needed to balance
my life out. She kept me on my toes and organized. She was a
very high stress person with a lot of tension and I mellowed
her out too. We had hit it off from the beginning, found what
I thought was love and gone on to be married and have our
daughter together, beautiful Zoe.

I even gave Tess the Laci test. I coined this after years of
finding the way to figure out if a relationship was worth
keeping or not. I would simply ask myself "If Laci walked
into my life and asked me to run away with her, would I
do it?"

If the answer was yes, then I should end my relationship. If
the answer was no, I finally found true love. With Tess, I
answered no so the next logical choice was to ask her to
marry me. What I didn't count on was finding Laci again...
through Facebook.

It started out as a congratulations on each others happiness,
which led to a meeting, which led to feelings which then led
to an intense make out session in a local restaurant. Every
feeling I had for Laci came flooding back to me. The strength

of love, the adoration, all of it; it was like a tidal wave crashing through me.

Tess was 3 months pregnant with Zoe at the time and I had a panic attack. A huge conflict of motivation, obligation and sense of duty overcame me and I actually felt guilt. Like an idiot I confessed everything to Tess the next day thereby destroying the trust in our relationship. Trust is all anyone has in a relationship and it's the one pillar everything else is based around. Mess with that and you end your world.

This did not happen amazingly. Tess is a very strong, independent person with very strong opinions on morals and ethics. I was certain she'd dump me, pregnant or not but she didn't. She made a conscious choice to forgive me, accept my temporary insanity plea and trust me again.

Ending things with Laci after promising her I would leave Tess for her resulted badly. There was anger, frustration and heartache. I was blocked on Facebook for a long time. A year in fact. I had all but lost any hope of ever hearing from Laci again. And then I got the strangest email.

Laci sent me a message on Facebook asking to be friends again. She was engaged again to some other sociopathic douche and just like last time, she was on the verge of ending it. He was just another neglectful, self serving, immature limp fish who had disappointed her for the last time with his philandering and mistreatment of her.

We quickly began a dialogue and although I told my wife Laci had emailed me, I also told her that I deleted the message and ignored her. That was obviously a lie. Tables had turned. Laci knew more about me and my situation than Tess did. It wasn't fair to her but she was also in the dark, which was better for her all around.

I started seeing Laci again. First it was innocent little coffee dates and movies. We went to see a horror film, something low budget and shot entirely hand held as was the Hollywood fad at the time and we maybe caught 20 minutes of a 90 minute movie between all the intense kissing we were doing.

It was the first week of October and I had always done something very elaborate for Halloween. Laci wanted to join me for Halloween, get a hotel and spend the entire day having sex. I was all about it but I knew there was no way I could wait that long. The engine in the back of my head that makes things happen started planning and plotting immediately on how to make this happen. Only problem was, she lived about an hour out of town and logistics were difficult to manage.

I would come back to this problem later, right now I had someone to kill and some new methods to try out.

I went to my neighborhood Home Depot to find what I needed and sure enough, in the plumbing section there they were; two galvanized steel pipes. I thought it might do to pick up some hockey tape while I was there in order to create a better grip on one side.

I rounded the aisle just in time to see a daddy daughter team shopping for plumbing accessories, no doubt for their original intended use. The little girl couldn't have been any older than five and had found the stick portion of a toilet plunger without its companion on the end. She wielded it like a sword and held a defensive pose, quite expertly I might add.

Ordinarily I'm somewhat irritated by children but when they do something stunningly mature for their age or endearing to my heart I can't help but smile and smile I did at this feisty little sweetheart who I hoped would be Zoe in 4 years.

The girl grinned sheepishly back at me. Her smile revealed her thoughts. She was smiling with a face that said "I'm a little embarrassed that you caught me but you seem to think it's cool so I'll return the devilish grin you're giving me." I think the young lady and I shared a moment just then.

I strolled out into the parking lot and got back into the comfy me shaped indent in the front seat of my maroon sedan. I wrapped the pipe ends in hockey tape for optimal gripping. Satisfied with this, I went home to relax and to set up my next victim.

The cool thing about a seven month old is that you can openly tell them anything and they can't rat you out. I needed that from my daughter, since anyone else I could spill to would be dialing nine one one before I finished. I knew I only had a limited amount of time before Zoes comprehension got to the level where that wouldn't fly so I got in as much talk time as possible in her early development when the words were just soothing sounds to get her used to the English language.

———

break.

I'm a huge fan of the Showtime series Dexter, as you may have guessed if you're at all familiar with the show. Dexter enjoys the sweet dark alone time of his own apartment since his TV girlfriend Rita and her two kids, Astor and Cody are not as tangled into his life as my family is with mine. I had to do with the sweet dark alone time of my basement computer office.

Once the child was snugly tucked away in her crib and my wife was sleeping peacefully, it sufficed perfectly for what I needed to do. My wife is certainly no sound sleeper, requiring ear plugs just to conk out and getting up several times during the night but we sleep apart so my disturbing her from getting up was never an issue.

Some people think that sleeping apart is detrimental to the relationship. I don't see how. I mean I'm only a serial killer, seeing my ex girlfriend on the side and my wife has no clue about it. But neither of those things has to do with the sleeping arrangements in our household. I sleep in the basement because I often stay up later than my wife and when we do sleep together, there's never enough room in a queen bed for two. Eventually the kicking and blanket hogging had us re-evaluate the importance of sharing a mattress.

I fired up my IP address blocker and launched two windows for my dual purpose. Keeping to my rules of never using the same account twice for anything, I opened a brand new email account. I stuck to the majors. Hotmail, Yahoo, Gmail. Something generic. When choosing a username it always reflected my new alias in some way. If I was an immigrant from Ireland looking for guys with a thing for redheads I'd use a username to the effect of Irishfirecream or something else just as apt.

Once the account had been created I used the second window to launch the dating site of choice. I switched that up to keep it interesting as well. Sometimes I would use a basic free service, and sometime I would use an elaborate pay service. It never mattered because women never have to pay to use those sites anyways. It's the homy retards on the other end who let their dicks dreams open their wallets.

On this night, a Thursday, I decided on a free site. Now photos are important. A photo of a girl that looks too professional gets overlooked because it reeks of spam bot. It also causes the guys to ask for more photos, which I would, of course, not have and would be forced to start from scratch.

A handy trick I use is to steal other women's photos from the same site, but in a different city. So if I posted my profile originating from say Portland, I would do a quick search in Nashville first and find a woman who I would genuinely be attracted to. Someone who doesn't come off as a total slut, but who also doesn't exude prude either. In this case I went ahead and chose the redhead from Ireland going out of country entirely for the photos.

Writing a woman's dating profile is very simple. You read enough and they all start to sound the same after awhile. I wrote delicately, sweetly, as a woman would write. I listed a few of the things my new persona was not interested in and made a few kind comments at the end and an invitation to message me.

This profile was listed looking for 'dating', which is much more manageable than 'intimate encounter'. When looking for dating I only had to sift through less than thirty emails throughout the day. But when putting 'intimate encounter' it's more like thirty messages per hour, sometimes more. That can be good or bad depending on what you're looking for.

I was looking for someone to match my needs for a new victim. I wanted a man who was financially stable, lived alone, didn't answer to too many people and might have some time off coming up. I got exactly what I was looking for.

Amongst the smart assed punks and the creepy old fellas who frankly, would be more suspicious of me if I gave them the time of day than not based on their appearances, was my target. A six foot'ish seemingly nice man who appeared clean cut, not overly good looking but not an ogre either and most importantly, fit for the profile.

We exchanged messages back and forth but when it came time to move in for the invite, another curve ball came my way. He wasn't available Friday, only Saturday. I had put in too much time with this asshole to start over and my mind began to race about how to fit it in.

I chose Fridays because I had a fake appointment with an imaginary psychiatrist who I told my wife I was seeing to sort out some of my issues, although I had already done that some time before. It was a very convenient and perfectly credible cover story though and I saw the merit in keeping the illusion going for the purpose of my late night freedom.

So every Friday I would leave the house, and prep for a kill while my wife was convinced my shrink was working his magic. I even added the special performance of seeming lighter and more relaxed when I walked back into the house. It was only partially an act since I did in fact feel good about my evening, just not in the way Tess quite expected.

Starting a kill on a Friday works on so many levels. For one thing, most people are not hard and fast expected to be anywhere on the weekend which gives me three days to clean up and tie up the loose ends. For another, I ordinarily need to skulk around doing my dirty work in the dead of night after Tess and Zoe are fast asleep. With all that night activity I get pretty bagged during the day so it's nice to not have career obligations on top of a lack of sleep.

I wasn't quite sure how to deal with my new friends schedule change. I thought to myself that starting over and slamming on the gas with a different profile entirely in order to stick to plan would have been the best idea. But I had already groomed this guy and felt profile mattered more than time of day.

I decided to leave it open and sleep on it, deciding what to do in the morning.

Friday morning came and my decision was made. I would scrap yesterdays escapade and start over fresh. I found some new photos of a girl from L.A. and whipped up an intimate encounter profile. Something quick and dirty and to the point. She was on the prowl and looking to hook up that very night, my chosen night.

Then something happened I did not expect; a pleasant surprise among the scads of emails from young douchebags with no appeal at all and some flaming rude comments at the ready. I got a message from Mr. Thursday.

It seemed that he was not only a liar but a wannabe player as well. He lied to my other dummy account about being tied up Friday and was seeking something with more immediate gratification for the time being. It was all I needed to see.

I flirted back and forth like it was an art form. Finally when enough messages had been exchanged and I felt comfortable with his comfort level I invited him in. It crossed my mind to use my other account to message him and entice him into this night as well just to watch him squirm but I would watch him squirm plenty in person.

I gave him step by step directions to my kill room without revealing an address and making sure to include the general excuses about the bus stop in front of the place and the lack of parking. He bought it hook line and sinker. The time was set. 7:00 pm.

My kill room was still perfectly set up from the last time, plastic sheeting hanging from the walls, on the floor and of course around my glorious table, duct tape sealing the seams to create a bubble to work within. I put that useless stun baton away and stretched my body out to limber up. I donned my mask, pulled my hood up and waited. The lights were still on inside the garage. It was 6:47 and I had a little time yet so I got myself psyched up for the main event.

Suddenly I heard the rumble of a car engine and sharply turned to see the wheel base of a Mazda slow and then continue. My adrenaline soared. That was him. The bastard was early and I know he had to have seen my feet at the very least. I decided to stick to the pattern anyway. I shut the lights all down and waited behind the curtain I had rigged up to shield me from sight; my two pipes in hand.

I ran entirely on sounds now. The cars engine silencing. The brief pause where all I could hear was the distant sound of main drag traffic lightly dancing in the background. Then the door opened, footsteps followed and then the car door slammed shut.

Another pause.

I could hear the crinkle of his clothing as he crouched to get under the door. He stood up and said "Hello?"

I froze. This was new. I've never heard anyone call out hello to a black empty room before. He assumed I was still here, and he was right. After all I had told him under my alias that there would be a guy using the garage for the weekend as a workshop.

I quickly took the mask off setting it on the weaker secondary table I used for my laptop. And without any other plan I began acting again.

"Hello?" I called back in a cheerful tone. I moved to the light switches and illuminated the room. "I'm Harry" I said pointedly, not sure what else to say exactly. "I'm a local film maker, preparing a set that's supposed to look like a serial killers little area here. You might have heard of my stuff. I'm the guy who put together the comedy feature at our local film festival."

"l haven't heard of that." replied the man who I will refer to from now on as Jim.

I went into super friendly mode, showed him my prop gun and how it wasn't real. I quickly mentioned that his date was running a little late and would be back in about twenty minutes. He said he would come back.

For twenty minutes I paced back and forth considering what to do, weighing the risks and the benefits. He could be on the phone to one of his friends revealing the address and telling them all about my set up. On the other hand he knows me so now I have an advantage over him and simultaneously, an obligation to use that advantage to remove him from the picture.

Still when my twenty minutes were up, I chickened out. As his car pulled up for the second time I whipped out my cell phone and in another grand performance pretended to talk to my alias over the phone. I delivered the bad news that tragically it looked like she wasn't going to be able to make it.

"I'm sorry bud, I don't know how long you had to drive to get here (27 blocks total, 10 minutes tops including lights) but it sounds like she's stuck in traffic and has no idea how long she'll be."

And with that, my victim left. He walked right out the door that should've been closing on his doom right then. I took

stock of my situation. I was standing in the middle of a
perfectly prepped kill room and was actually going to let this
go down as strike 2. I already had the room set up and the
whole night was mine to do with as I pleased so I jumped
back online to find someone who was willing to drop everything and head over right away.

My new account which I had just created that morning had
clear over 200 messages from all sorts of people. After
twenty five minutes of perusing I still had nothing when my
twice escaped victim sent me a message. My immediate reply
was a huge apology and an offer to reschedule for the
next day.

His reply was to come over again that very night. He didn't
live far and didn't want to waste his night any more than I
wanted to waste mine. I stared at the laptop screen,
unmoving for half an hour deciding. Humming and hawing
over the details. Finally I went for it. I typed a message back
with a quick apology for the delay and an invitation to come
back. I meant business.

Crouched, poised, I had a whole new plan. No mask needed
this time. Just pretending to be poking around at the back of
the set and then WHAM! I would slam him unconscious and
his survival would be a bonus, but not necessary. He played
into it perfectly. He reappeared through the garage door and
I soon followed.

"l guess I'm just a glutton for punishment" he shrugged.

"You have no idea."

The room filled with the echo of the pipe crashing into the
back of his skull as I could feel my predator self take over.
That one single motion was the end all be all. I had
committed now and there was no going back. The jig was up

and it was kill or get arrested for aggravated assault with a deadly weapon, maybe even attempted murder.

I won't go to jail for an almost. But the son of a bitch didn't drop like the sack of potatoes I was expecting. Are you serious? I asked myself. I continued thwacking Jim over the head repeatedly but it only seemed to fuel his adrenaline too.

He began screaming at the top of his lungs. "Police! Police! Police!" and I just about shat my pants. My fury doubled and I blasted him so hard blood spattered everywhere, but primarily on me. He hit the floor but was still conscious.

Just like they all do, he offered money immediately. I always find this a little degrading for both my victim and myself. Like I couldn't just kill them and take it anyway. No please Mr. victim, give me some petty cash from your wallet and run along to the cops only to lead them back here. Ridiculous.

I paused for a minute. "You promise?" I said.

"Yes just please stop hitting me, Oh my skull." Was his reply. And then in the instant he had to think about it I wailed on him again. Despite receiving several mortal blows to the head, the shock and adrenaline of the situation gave him the fire to fight back a little.

"I've had enough of this." He said as he feebly and dizzily tried to grab the pipe away from me. My anger resurged, I wrestled it from him and that was the last straw for me. I pulled my hunting knife from it's sheath and watching the shock on his face as he saw the blade, I thrust it into his gut. His reaction was pure Hollywood. The lurch forward with the grunt was dead on TV movie of the week.

I didn't even notice the garage door was still part open. Wasn't I suppose to close that? Will I never learn?

No one came. No one rustled, not even from across the alley. My little notices that I sent out to the neighbors about shooting thrillers here did their job and no one paid attention, assuming it was a scene or something. Oh it was a scene alright.

Jim moaned and groaned. I plunged the knife deep into his neck. Days after the event I would reflect on this and wish I had tricked him by offering to call an ambulance if he just gave me his debit pin code before I sliced open his jugular. Maybe I'll save that for the next victim since they never seem to just fall the fuck asleep like they're supposed to.

I let him bleed out right there on the floor, away from the plastic sheeting specifically put up to avoid that sort of thing. But hey I had bigger problems. I had no real idea if a jogger, a dog walker, an unconvinced neighbor or some other random individual had actually called the cops, just as a precaution.

I was standing there covered in blood. It was all over my face, my hoody, my coat and my jeans. I was holding the murder weapon in my hand standing over what would be in moments, a corpse and not nearly enough time to make it go away.

I got my things ready and did the only thing I could do. I waited. I waited for a sign on what to do next. I waited for the fast approach of sirens as a cue to leave and come up with a damn good story for later. I waited and I was rewarded with silence. Sweet sweet silence. I got lucky. No one freaked out, no one reacted, no one inadvertently witnessed it and no one called the boys in blue. I was home free.

I assessed my situation and went to town on my improvised solution. I had a dead guy that needed processing so that's what I did. I processed him.

I remember thinking as I hoisted this giant up onto my table that I should really stick to smaller guys from now on. This guy was at least 2 inches taller than I was and maybe a couple of pounds heavier, and I'm no shrimp.

But I got his dead carcass up on that table and I figured that since I went through all this trouble and made all this mess that I would have to clean up, I got my game processing kit out which contained a butcher knife for the hefty meat, a fillet knife for smaller works, a skinner which might come in handy for scalping the skull, and a serrated saw for the bones. A pair of scissors there was also and a cutting board. I had the cleaver there from another order I had placed.

I decided the best course would be to go from the feet up. First things first, I pulled out his wallet and keys and placed them on my computer table. Then I used the scissors to cut his pants apart and pull them away. I had my 45 gallon steel drum host to a contractor grade hefty bag where I was putting all the items. I cut the shirt off too but left the underwear. I don't need to see my kills dead junk hanging out while I'm trying to work.

I poked and prodded the joints to find the path of least resistance. I began cutting the legs off at the knees, all in one piece. I didn't even bother to take his shoes or socks off. The knife went through flesh like it was nothing. I was surprised at how utterly non resilient human tissue can be. Even the tendons and ligaments separated cleanly.

There was almost no blood. Not surprising since the grand majority of it was pooled on the floor, thankfully soaked up primarily by Jims jacket which had come off during our struggle.

I put the severed leg in the trash and moved on to the thigh which was essentially the same routine, only thicker, more fatty. I noticed that it wasn't nearly as horrendous as the media made it look on TV or in movies. Dismembering a human body was a relatively unexciting event. But I had my ways of making it more fun. I sang to myself as I worked, talked to myself, reflected on the new tools I would get to make the next one easier.

I took the arms off at the elbow joint and used the scissors to cut off fingertips for added confusion in identifying the body. This man was very common with no special internal additions to speak of.

Severing the head was also a simple matter and going through the vertebrae in the back of the neck didn't take much at all by going through connective tissue.

The torso was surprisingly heavy all by itself and I cut that in two across the diaphragm. Human intestines just look like one long roll of uncooked sausage as opposed to the grue-some millage of stringy nastiness they appear to be on film. I was surprised. Funny sounds and pressure releases took place on my table as the torso sank.

Once the body was in bags, I started my cleanup process. I took down the plastic walls from my bubble which surpris-ingly had almost no spatter on them. Then I started to roll the plastic on the table up and to my chagrin, noticed it had very little effect in keeping the blood off the tables steel surface. I soldiered on, cleaning up all of the plastic. I tore my green cloth backdrop down and placed it over the larger blood pools on the floor after I picked up the soaked coat and trashed it.

The green backdrops went into the trash next and then I began my stain removal process. I had two bottles of pure ammonia that I dabbed into paper towels to wipe away small stains. The spatter was everywhere. There were dozens of small spots on the floor and tiny streaks on the walls and big door. I wiped them all away. The great thing about ammonia is that even if the stain won't completely wipe away, it destroys the sample so that no DNA can be processed. It also eats fingerprints like acid. It's only downside is the fumes, which I didn't smell so much as feel like a cold winter breeze shooting its way through my sinuses.

I kept away from it and wore masks whenever possible. I wiped my table clean, scrubbed the areas on the floor that needed it, wiped my computer table down and noticed a few tiny spots had made it onto my laptop. I was not impressed but knew they would be easy to spot clean.

Next time, the whole room gets bubbled, not just the half for my kill room. I had used a plastic sheeting normally chosen to cover living room furniture when painting walls, but it obviously didn't suffice. This time I used a single layer of mid grade quality stuff. Next time I would double layer the high grade material for sure.

When I got finished I looked down in horror at the sheer level of blood staining my clothes from head to toe. I couldn't walk back into the house like this. I mean I had extra clothes in my car I could change into, that wasn't the point. But surely there would be a smell and I couldn't get all the blood off my face, not all of it.

My phone rang. The familiar buzzing of it's vibrate setting going off. The caller ID showed it was Tess calling. What could I do? I answered.

"Hi baby, what's up?"

Not much. Where are you?"

"I'm just leaving the gym hun."

"The gym closes at nine."

I checked my watch hurriedly, it showed 9:57 pm. My mind raced. I couldn't get caught in a lie. Not again.

"What are you talking about babe? It closes at ten."

"The big gym by our place?"

And there was my window. I had switched gyms when we moved to our new house so it sorted itself out as I jumped back in to play the game. "No, my old gym babe."

"I thought you cancelled that membership a month ago."

'I procrastinated…" as I do tend to do quite often. "and did it a few weeks ago but I still have a couple weeks this month that are paid for so I figured I'd take advantage since it takes an hour to cross town anyway."

My wife is not stupid. It takes a lot to convince her of an elaborate lie. When she caught me surfing internet dating sites, I spun this quick tale of how I was just research an article on online dating I got through a free lance website. Fortunately for me, I really was a member of the free lance site already and could prove that part.

The next part was much harder. She wanted proof upon proof. I had to manufacture an entire person which is a lot more hassle than it sounds. I created a fake employer, ran out to get a prepaid cell phone and then hired an actor to do a role play on the phone with me, on speaker so Tess could hear it. Then I had him leave a voicemail message as this person so that if she called the number it would sound legit.

I went through great lengths to bring my wife over to the comfortable belief I wasn't cheating on her, but me hiding anything was the problem. Even safely believing in my fidelity didn't matter next to the dishonesty of hiding the article from her in the first place. And so our trust issues flared up again. Now every conversation was an interrogation. Not just a simple question where she could take my answer at my word. There had to be back checking involved. So I waited for her response to my explanation and after a short breath…

"Ok, well listen on your way home can you pick up a case of ready made baby formula at Shoppers?"

"Will do. Anything else?" In my mind I begged for her not to ask me to get her a late night latte. That's all I needed was to walk into a Starbucks in mismatching attire, dried blood across my face and hands. That sort of thing people notice, even if they feel too awkward to ask questions.

'No, but I'll probably be in bed by the time you get home. I'm so tired." She said with a yawn. Finally a break. A dark silent home to come to where I can go straight into the basement, throw my coat, hoody, pants, shoes, socks and shirt straight into the laundry and shower any remnants off of me.

"Fantastic. I'll see you tomorrow then."

"Kay, bye."

I packed up my laptop bag and then opened the garage door, half expecting a team of police cruisers to be waiting outside, but the alley was empty and silent save for the Mazda parked in the driveway. I took the keys and got in. A fucking manual transmission. I had never learned how to drive them but necessity is the mother of invention after all. I probably stalled the damn thing a good ten times before enough trial and error got me to the point where I could manage to get the stupid thing inside the garage.

I laid a plastic sheet across the hatchback floor and put the body bags in the trunk. At least the car was clean and empty. After a quick search I found Jims cell phone, turned it off to avoid pings sent from the police to track it and made sure there was no GPS turned on either. I locked up the garage, went out to my car under cover of night and changed clothes, stuffing the blood soaked ones into my duffle bag. I changed shoes as well. Another glance at my watch gave me the realization the store would be closed by the time I got there and sure enough, by the time I reached the other side of town I was way too late to buy formula. It was the last of my worries.

I decided to wake up early and run out to the store to grab the formula before the baby woke up but I was so bagged from the events of the night before that I overslept and had to make up something to the warden about them being out of stock last night when I went which allowed me to make the trip Saturday morning.

I had a pretty normal Saturday. Watching the kid so Tess could get some personal stuff tended to, having a bit of a break from the constant supervision of a young infant, cute as she was.

Zoe had always been exceptionally adorable and it wasn't just us biased parents who thought so. Everyone at the hospital was of the same opinion and every time Tess ran errands, the ladies at the bank would swoon over Zoe like she was the second coming of Christ in a female package. She charmed everyone who met her. She softened the hardened selfish prick that was Tess' father, and won over several others who until meeting Zoe, had not been "kid people" at all. The final confirmation of that was when mother and daughter had gone to get her first professional pictures taken and even the people at the photo studio who dealt with children all day every day noted how exceptionally happy and easy going she was.

Zoe was born mellow. When other kids are throwing tantrums in public she stares at them with a questioning as to what the hell could be wrong with them. She loves going places and was very early to alertness. When other babies were dough eyed or utterly confused, she was looking around, tracking everything and looking at people directly with curiosity.

She's a wonderful baby, an angel that we were spoiled to have with such an easy disposition. I really hope she doesn't end up like me. I watched an episode of Dexter where the flash-back showed his father showing Dexter CAT scans of a human brain. He identified the differences between a serial killers brain and a normal persons brain.

Up until I saw that I was convinced that what I was, was my own decision, my own path but now I truly wondered if I had little choice at all, and if genetics play a bigger role than I thought.

Logically then it should have occurred to me that those traits have a possibility of being passed to my offspring. I do have hope for Zoe though. My parents are certainly not like me so there's no guarantee on generational transition, and she is also half Tess and I've never seen such empathy, moral code or ethical sturdiness as I have in her.

Quite the odd couple Tess and I. On a couple of occasions we even discussed my apparent total lack of empathy and it troubled her greatly. She asked me a long series of probing and somewhat leading questions to see if I would give her the answer she desired but I never did.

"When you see news stories of people going through tremendous grief or strife, do you feel bad for them?"

"No.'

'Do you ever think about what it would be like if that were your family in that situation?"

"It's never crossed my mind." was my answer and it continued like this until Tess was satisfied her husband couldn't feel much of anything at all I imagine. I did calm her fears though by at least reassuring her that I did care very much about her and Zoe and that neither of them would ever feel unloved.

I do love my daughter very much. She brings me great joy, and I love playing games with her. If anyone ever threatened her happy innocent existence in any way I would kill them, cut the body up and make it disappear. Most people say that about their children, only I actually mean it literally.

Sunday was all set up for more family merriment, much like the Saturday before it. I began to get itchy though and wanted to move on to the next part of my overall plan for Jim. I woke up at the crack of dawn, 5:00 am and left the house. Neither of the ladies would be up for another three hours and I had a person to erase.

I drove across town to the South side, not for the kill room this time, but for the home of my victim. I found his place without pause, parked in front of the building, careful to examine surroundings and make sure that there was no video surveillance. It was still early morning and comings and goings were common in the area.

I wore my hoody to cover my head and face, and my gloves to leave prints out of the situation entirely. My shoes had just come out of the dryer and were spotless. They would leave no imprints anywhere inside the apartment. I used his keys to enter the building, cautiously watching for video surveillance and strolled down the hallway until I found the door I needed.

I paused for a moment, better not to take chances. I knocked first, just in case for whatever reason, there was someone inside. There wasn't and slowly I entered the place closing and locking the door behind me. A simple one bedroom apartment. Somewhat clean save for a few dishes left out. It represented a single man perfectly. Motor cycle gear, a big screen TV, a computer desk, a nice barbecue and some online gaming machinery.

I found cash on the dresser which quickly found its way into my wallet. I searched drawers and shelves for anything else of interest, putting everything back as it was. Then I sat down at the computer desk. I wasn't sure what I would find. I was hoping some basic searches would yield passwords or something but Jim had done me one better. He left himself signed in to everything. Messenger, outlook express, his online dating profile and his facebook all had the passwords auto saved.

I couldn't have had an easier time. I changed the auto response on his email to say he had decided to run away with the woman he hooked up with on Friday to go on a two month vacation to the Caribbean. I changed the status on his facebook account to reflect the change and then I proceeded to delete his online dating profile. Judging by his email content it seemed he was on several sites at once so that trail would go cold real quickly.

My phone rang. It was Tess again asking where I was. I said I had gone to my parents to pick up a few tools for working on the downstairs bathroom and that I would be back in an hour. Conversation over. I had an after thought. What if the police ever did track this back to me and checked my cell phone records? They would see the towers my phone picked its signal up from and notice I was in the area. If the garage I rented wasn't already a few streets away that might be a problem.

I packed Jims laptop up and took it with me. I also took his multifunction printer and threw it into a dumpster because the email I sent him with directions to my kill room had been printed on it and it wouldn't do to have that be recoverable by the police. But I did find something in the printer that would help. A letter to his insurance company with a clear unmarked signature on white background.

It was one last gift from the dead. I could easily use that to forge a bill of sale for the car. If the authorities ever questioned me about it I could corroborate my own story. "Yeah officer it was the strangest thing. This guy approaches me on the street and tells me he met this phenomenal woman, a real sugar mamma who is going to take care of him and that he doesn't need his car anymore. So he asks me how much I have on me and when I tell him I've only got twenty three bucks, he says 'Ok deal' and I end up with a free car."

Armed with my new toys and info I headed home. My next problem was what to do with the body. I mean it's not like I had an ocean to dump it in, or a boat for that matter. What did that leave? When you live in a land locked city what are your options for making two hundred and thirty pounds of dead human go away?

Incineration. I had looked into buying an actual batch incinerator. Something with the pressure and heat needed to get the job done. The problem with those are that they cost upwards of five thousand dollars to acquire and I wouldn't be in a position to make that purchase for another month or two. I had a jerry can of gasoline in my trunk and a steel drum though. Close enough.

Monday morning and I had some free time to myself, at least until about 4:30 in the afternoon when the wife expected me to be back home. To keep the illusion of my day job up, I would leave earlier on Mondays to pretend I had to be in a Monday morning meeting.

I went straight to my kill room. I lined my trunk with plastic sheeting and stuffed the body bags in. I laid the drum across the back seat and stuffed my garbage bags into it to save space and extra trips. I took everything to my parents house. They were gone during the day and had a nice fenced back yard for privacy.

My arms were very sore. Maybe the athletic event leading into the weekend had been quite jarring but I was experiencing shooting pain that was clearly the result of pinched nerves in my back. I didn't have the time or money to see a chiropractor but I would use the massage chair I gave my wife for Christmas one year several times later that night.

In the meantime though, everything was a chore. Lifting the barrel, lifting the bags out of the trunk; they were all accompanied by soreness and agitation. At some points my arms would recoil sharply in exhaustion from pushing them no further than what felt like an average hoisting.

I doused the first bag which contained the torso pieces in gasoline after dropping it into the barrel. I lit a match and tossed it in. The instant whoosh of flames consuming flammable liquid exploded from the top and the burn began. I had placed the barrel squarely in the center of the yard. It was broad daylight but everything was sealed in bags so no one could see anything, especially not the burning process.

I've heard that there is no smell like that of a burning fleshy person. If I had a sense of smell I may have taken note but I lack that particular member of the five sense group so you won't get any dramatic descriptions from me.

I imagine it smells like barbecue steak mixed with singed hair. When you cut up a person you realize we are really no different than animals. We're just sacks of meat at the end of the day. The internal muscles and tissues of the human body look a whole lot like steak actually. In fact, if properly trimmed and packaged, I believe most people would have a hard time telling them apart.

Maybe they taste different but I never felt the compulsion to cross that line. I could see the curiosity that Dahmer had and I understand the mentality behind why he did it, I just don't think that way and I'm not about to eat any meat that's been dead and sitting out for days, regardless of the source. It tends to change how one views a sirloin when it comes to the table though.

I checked on my burning waste and added more gas. Not straight out of the jerry can of course, I'm not up for any Darwin awards. I poured some into a coffee cup and dumped accordingly. I repeated that three times when I realized it wasn't doing anything. The pain in my arms became merely the start of my problems. My biggest issue now was the complete lack of effectiveness this method of disposal had.

As if that weren't bad enough I heard sirens. Now in my kill rooms neighborhood sirens are customary and you know it's time to worry when you don't hear them on a nightly basis. But in this nice sweet little schoolyard area, sirens mean something significant. Someone spotted the smoke and called the fire department. I now had two very big reasons to put the fire out.

I doused the fire in water extinguishing it immediately. The smoke dissipated and almost as if the fire crew knew exactly what was happening, the sirens stopped. It could have been a massive coincidence but I heavily doubted it. All I knew was that having the fire crew pull up to the house and start poking around was not an option. Granted a charred and cut up torso looks somewhat similar to a couple pieces of big beef but any closer inspection would expose me and that wouldn't do.

When the smoke cleared I found that the bag had melted and some of the edges were charred but for the most part, the body was still in tact, some of the skin hadn't even been cooked. I knew there was no way the organs were affected. It would take a week to burn the waste unrecognizable at this pace and use more gas than I could afford. So I re-bagged everything, loaded it back into the car and took it back to the kill room.

Realizing that incineration was out completely I had to change strategies. I decided to cut the body into smaller pieces and dump it in the river that ran straight through middle of the city creating an impromptu border between the North and South sides of town. I didn't have time for that the same afternoon, it would have to wait a day or two.

After the days activities were complete I headed home a little earlier. I played with Zoe, watching her while Tess took a shower and relaxed. I fed the child dinner, gave her a bath and then it would be time for her to go to sleep. Zoe slept straight through the night only a week after she was born. The kid loves sleeping and by seven months on the planet she was out for twelve straight hours every night starting at 7:30 pm. Like I said, lucky.

As Tess settled in on the living room couch to watch her evening programs I jumped on the computer. Laci was online and I began chatting with her. At first it was cordial, loosely discussing plans to get together again. I was looking forward to having her again and I know she felt the same way. We were both getting impatient and it was showing in our conversations.

Neither one of us had experienced sex nearly as good as each others in the eight years we had been apart. Her relationships were with pathetic losers who preferred playing online games over actual human affection and when they did get in the mood, they lasted for only a couple minutes at a time. I never understood how a guy can cum so easily with so little self control lasting less than ten minutes in a session. I always loved taking my time and Laci felt the same way.

My first marriage was heated all the way through but this meant the fighting was just as intense as the love making and it became too much to handle. Besides I got married for all the wrong reasons the first time, getting into a relationship just because I thought I was ready. I was very young, only twenty one at the time and too stupid to realize the truth. My wife was less attractive than me, and a little overweight but cute.

At any rate it didn't last. The second best sexual experience I ever had was with a Laotian girl I was essentially using for my rebound, but of course she didn't see it that way. She was under the impression we were a long term thing and we might have been if I wasn't so screwed up. She could hold her own in the marathons and would actually say (almost out of breath) after we were done "How can anyone go for three hours straight?"

So when Laci popped up on the instant messenger inviting me to her place for a late night rendezvous I did everything in my power to make it happen. I knew I would need to wait until Tess was in bed so I could safely sneak out. I could easily spend the night at Laci's house since I could pass off not being there in the morning as getting an early start.

But even though Tess was tired and wanting to go to bed early, it just didn't happen. She stayed up, delaying my departure and I knew there was a solid hour and a half drive time to get to Laci's. As Tess was going to bed I took my computer bag into the living room telling her I was going to stay up and write for awhile. She accepted that with no reserve and went to bed.

In two minutes I was out the door. I jumped into the car and headed out to Laci's as fast as I could. Too fast in fact. I was pulled over for speeding on the freeway. I did another round of top notch acting pretending to give a shit about breaking the posting limit and begged for him to go easy on me. He gave me a ticket anyway but at least it was less than half the price it could have been and I also appreciated how quick he was about it. I was back on the road in five minutes flat.

I remember thinking how hilarious and dramatically ironic it was that the cop had pulled over a cold blooded murderer who had a dismembered body in his rented garage not too far away and had no clue what was going on. He just did his duty and took off. Now every time I pass a police car on the road I chuckle to myself.

I got to Laci's without further incident. She let me inside dressed in her pajamas and no sooner had I dropped my bag on the floor than we were making out intensely. We moved to her bedroom and shut the door to keep her dogs out. We kissed passionately in juicy anticipation of what was coming next. She lay on her bed and opened the pajamas to reveal a sexy set of white lingerie style underwear. The bottoms were a thong which always gets me insanely turned on.

Laci looked better than I had ever remembered her. A decade ago at the tender age of twenty four she was gorgeous but still not as fine as she looked this very night in question. She had been hitting the gym, gone tanning to prepare for her vacation and had taken up the hobby of belly dancing. I have never been a fan of scrawny girls. In my opinion if you can see ribs poking through the skin the woman needs a hefty helping of cheeseburgers very badly. Laci was beautiful, sensual with curves in all the right places. Now she was the ideal textbook form of what a woman should look like with the added skill of how to rotate her hips in ways most women only dream they could.

Her large deep green eyes stared seductively into mine and I couldn't resist her even if I tried, not that I would want to try. Being with her took on the pace of quickly catching up to how we used to be.

Laci and I explored each other for a good two hours that night trying several positions, all of them making both of us crazy. I was free to suck on various parts of her body and go down on her for as long as she could take it before needing me inside her again. The way she felt, the way she tasted, all so familiar and so amazing to have again. She came to orgasm four times before I let myself get to the same place and when we were done there was no describing the contentment we experienced.

I laid there next to her gently stroking her hair and back. I examined the tattoo on her left shoulder blade, the one I had designed for her in college. It was a celtic knot style cross with vines intertwined within it; a beautiful piece, inked by a real master. Her second; placed on the back of her neck acquired at the same location, was done by someone clearly less experienced since its lines were not perfect and the shading slightly out of balance. It still looked good from a few feet away but this close up it didn't compete with the first.

She remembered mine too. The one on my left shoulder I had gotten while dating her all those years ago. It had since been retouched and I was physically much bigger from filling out as an adult and frequent trips to the gym. Maybe it was me being of a larger stature than my thin teenage self of the past, but she seemed smaller this time. My other two tattoos were more recent and new additions to her.

Some of our past together was as clear as day to Laci. Other elements were lost to her. She had gone on a vacation to a third world tropical country and brought back with her a virus that attacked her brain. She had been ill for two years as a result and it could have ended much worse with some sort of organic brain dementia or even death coming for her.

She escaped with her health and her faculties, as well as this smoking hot new body.

I fell asleep next to her and when I awoke in the morning, she had to be at work in the city, whereas I had nowhere to be. So I slept in, she left me a spare key and when I was ready I got ready to leave. Her dogs woke up to greet me. They are small annoying little things that she treats as if they were human children, which I never understood but could easily respect since for years they were the only constant source of unconditional love and acceptance in her world.

In my opinion, a dog is something roughly the size of a German shepherd that you can actually wrestle with and take on walks without fear that a bird of prey will snatch it up like a squirrel and run it off to feed it to its young, but that's just me. These two uppity things would bark at any average Joe walking down the street and I couldn't wait to get out of there.

Laci had left the TV on so I turned it off, thinking that it would obviously be a tremendous waste of energy since I highly doubted a dog could get anything out of watching The View. I packed up my things, and left her spare key under a statue on her front porch before I took off for the day. I had work to do.

———

break.

It was time to assess the situation again. I had a hatchback with body parts in the trunk locked inside a garage I still had to sweep clean. I had waste to dispose of and tracks to erase. I had no idea who this guy had talked to in the interim periods between his first arrival at my lair and his last, so for all I knew some friend of his out there could even have the exact address or at the very least detailed descriptions of how to get there.

If I ever figured out a safe, quick way of rendering my victims unconscious at another location without witnesses or forensic evidence left behind, I would do that. But for now this system was fine as long as I stuck to strict adherence of the plan. I headed straight for my kill room to deal with my mess.

First things first, I grabbed breakfast from a Dennys that was just up the street from my sanctuary. My moons-over-my-hammy was especially delicious and I just had to stop by a 7-11 to pick up a chocolate milk and a large French vanilla latte. This meal would keep me satisfied for at least a couple hours. I made sure to pick up some snacks for the day as well.

When I arrived on the street of my kill room I approached cautiously, as always just in case. As each time prior there was no fanfare of police and ambulance gathered around the front or the back. No one had accidentally found anything and called it in. No weird smells were emitting from the place and very well shouldn't be considering everything was sealed and still fresh.

I got inside and prepped for what my day would be like. The nights rest had numbed the great majority of my nerve pain and I felt fine to continue. I began by taking the bags out of the Mazda and placing them on the floor next to my butcher table. I double sheeted the table this time, placed my processing kit, my cleaver and the galvanized pipe at one end, my ammonia cleaning supplies and paper towels on the other. I placed plastic sheeting around the table on the floor as well and moved the steel drum over within leaning distance with a brand new empty hefty bag in it to catch the waste.

The next step was to prep myself. I wouldn't allow any blood and guts to get on me today. I used some of my plastic sheeting and duct tape to fashion a makeshift apron for myself. I picked up new much higher grade plastic abrasive cleaner resistant gloves and then duct taped two grocery bags around my shoes to keep them clean also. I wore a basic white painters mask to keep fumes away from me and take some of the edge off the ammonia smell.

I picked up the first bag and set it on the table. I put my cutting board on the table, to prevent my knives from accidentally puncturing or tearing holes in my plastic sheeting which I suspected may have played a role in drenching my table surface last time. I had previously closed the bags by twisting the ends and wrapping the tightest part with duct tape so this time I just cut them open with the short knife.

I took out one of the arms. It was stiff and cold, rigor mortis having set in by now. It was also quite brisk outside today since it was fall heading into winter. I was grateful for the temperature though since my outfit was warm and I would be doing quite a bit of physical activity today.

I chose the butcher knife to start out with and simply shaved the meat from the bone in a downward motion. I didn't bother getting every single shred, since I knew that once dumped in the river, it would rot off in a timely fashion anyway. When it was cleared, each slab looked like a cutlet sitting on the table.

I put each chunk on the cutting board and used the fillet knife to slice them into even smaller pieces. When I was satisfied with my medallion sized portions, I tossed them into the garbage bag. Very little mess was made at first.

I repeated the process with the legs, thighs and upper arms. Routinely shaving the meat off them, placing the bones in a pile and filleting the meat into small pieces before tossing them into the bag. When the bag got somewhat heavy to lift easily, I closed it off in the same fashion as the originals and got a new one.

Once in a while I would take a break, check my email, answer a few phone calls, check the status of my ebay page and have a bag of chips. I got a message from Laci on Facebook commenting on how hot the night was and how she was looking forward to the next time. I fantasized about the night before and how Laci had been a total porn star in the sack. I was incredibly lucky. When I realized two hours had passed I decided to get the rest of the waste dealt with as soon as possible so I could take as much of the afternoon off as possible.

Every couple of body parts, I would need to clean and sharpen my knives since they were doing a lot of work going through so much material. I decided to do the head next. I sliced the face off in several different pieces, cut the ears and lips up so that again, they couldn't be visually identified. This way if someone did see it floating in a river, they would think nothing of it anyway.

Once the flesh was removed, I used the pipe to knock out the teeth, eliminating dental records as a form of ID. I broke the jaw after that and used the scissors to cut the ligaments, ripping the jaw clean from the head in it's multiple pieces held together only by the tissue at this point. I used the knife to destroy the eyes as well and then rammed the pipe into the side of the skull to bust it open. At this point it was fueled only by a curiosity to see the human brain live and in person since I had never seen it before.

I realized I was spending too much time on the head and tossed it into a new hefty bag to move on. Next came the two heavy torso pieces. My arm pain flared up hoisting them to the table and then subsided by simply mentally pushing it out of the way. I began with the lower portion. I removed the intestines first, carved out the reproductive organs and anything else taking up space. Then I shaved the meat off the hip bones for as much would come off.

Removing the skin and flesh in the back was easy. These were the chunks I tried to burn the first time around so the skin was charred in some places making it more stiff in some places and easy to cut. I hacked off the ass cheeks and marveled at how fatty they were for such a slim person. I immediately thought of the movie Alive and how well the rugby team must have feasted on this part of the human body while trapped in the Andes. But the freezer burn from the bodies being in the snow and frozen solid might have ruined the experience. Well that and the trauma of realizing you're eating a dead person but that never entered my thinking at all. Meat is meat after all. It all tastes like beef or chicken.

Once that was processed, I moved on to my final piece, the upper torso. I started with shaving the outside, taking all of the skin, muscle and fat in single passes, like I was carving a turkey. In fact once everything else had been removed, I was surprised at how closely the chest cavity resembles the overall shape of a turkey.

This was the messy portion. All of the blood that hadn't come out was inside this piece, trapped in the lungs, still close to the heart. It dumped out onto the table, not quite enough to overflow to the floor or anything but messy nonetheless. I used a knife to cut all the tissue around the inside edge of the rib cage in order to free any remaining organs. The lungs, the heart and the liver all came out. I cut those up too before trashing them.

It reminded me of emptying a pumpkin for Halloween. Somehow every single event in life would have a whole new level of perspective to it. Carving a pumpkin and spilling its guts would now carry a double meaning. So would slicing up a steak, carving a Thanksgiving turkey or laying plastic down to prepare for painting the family room.

This experience changed my sense of place in the world forever. I felt stronger, somehow above other people. I felt like the proud owner of a very dark secret that no one would ever be in on. Things that I said to people would carry double entendres like they hadn't before. "Oh honey work was murder today." would be more literal than Tess would ever know.

When the body was dealt with I used paper towels to soak up much of the blood spill on the table so it wouldn't flow onto unprotected floor in the clean up process. My makeshift outfit went into a separate trash bag, one designated for secondary waste, not body parts. All table plastic and surrounding plastic got rolled up and tossed accordingly. At first it appeared my double sheeting on the table did its job but upon final reveal, it turned out I needed to scrub with the stain remover again. High grade stuff next time, for sure

I felt good about this. My plan now involved simply waiting for dark to come so I could visit a bridge. I opened the garage door, satisfied that nothing conspicuous was showing to the outside and unlocked my car, which I had parked closer to the back door this time for easy transfer. I laid new plastic in my car trunk and placed the new bags in one at a time. I closed up shop and headed for home.

It's an interesting feeling, driving around town with what used to be a human body bagged up in your trunk. No one has any idea they are stopped at a light right next to a serial killer with what could very well be one of their friends now sacks of meat parts in a hidden compartment. It made me wonder, in all my ten years of driving around, had I ever unknowingly passed a vehicle or sat parked at a red light next to someone just like I would be one day? It blew my mind.

I stuck to the posted speed limits, signaled when I changed lanes and didn't push any yellow lights whatsoever. I'm convinced that car insurance companies would get exceedingly rich from not paying claims and hospital traffic would slow to a crawl on major holidays if everyone drove as if they had a dead man in their trunk and a mortal fear of going to jail for twenty to life in the event they ever got pulled over and a police man decided to check their cars contents.

I got home without incident and went through my evening routine with ease. I hopped on the instant messenger to find Laci online. Only this conversation was not a happy one at all, it had taken a terrible turn for the worse. She was horribly depressed from reflecting on her past relationship situations and behaving erratically. She said she couldn't continue to see me because she was messed up and didn't want to put that on me, even though I expressly said to her that her and I could take things at whatever pace she felt comfortable with.

But it was more than that. Laci had discovered her ex husband met the clinical definition of a sociopath. The epiphany didn't come from consulting a psychiatrist, it came from finding a detailed article on the internet that outlined what male sociopaths do to the women they shack up with. In it she found all of his most redeeming qualities. Chronic pathological lying, using and abusing his partner, scamming everyone around him, treating other people with a total lack of respect or regard for their well being. What really pushed her over the edge was reading all the traits of women who usually fall for people like this and brought the problem onto herself. She was certain there were several things terribly wrong with her and tonight that had spiraled into contemplating suicide.

I was completely taken by surprise and had no idea what to do. This wasn't her usual bummed out attitude when reflecting on the years wasted with the idiots who couldn't appreciate her: both her ex husband and the boyfriend she had shortly after whom she had recently dumped for neglecting her and mistreating her much the same way. This was different. She was repeating back to me something I had said about how those who threaten suicide usually don't mean it unless they have a specific plan laid out.

That's when I panicked. She talked about pills, wondering what four would do and I remember thinking it depended entirely on what the pill was, the difference between sickness and death. I couldn't take chances. I begged her not to do it and used every phrase to dissuade her, until the words "too late" popped onto my screen.

I did the only thing I could think of that was left. I picked up my phone and dialed 911.

"911 emergency."

"Hi, I've just been chatting online to a friend who has threatened suicide."

"Ok what's your name sir?"

"Darren Ascot." It was obviously not my real name but that was irrelevant.

"And your friends name?"

'Laci Barret."

"And where are you sir?"

"I'm in Bloomington heights."

"And where is she?"

"She lives in Whetstone."

'How long have you known her?"

"Ten years.'

'Did she say why she's doing this or how?"

"She didn't specify why." which was true. She didn't say and my guesses were still only assumptions. "She talked about pills."

"Do you have her address?" I answered with the exact numbered address of where she lived. "Ok we're sending people out right now."

"Thank you." Just in case Laci was still awake I got back on the instant messenger and typed in 'I just called 911 .' She responded shocked and appalled. She said I was being ridiculous and I asked her what else she could possibly expect me to do under the circumstances. The next message was hilarious.

'You are adding to my stress level' to which I could only reply…

'YOUR stress level?' She was emotional and crashing and it was completely understandable. Her ex husband fit the sociopath profile draining her of all her self esteem, leaving her wondering if she was an alien or something. To follow it up her most recent boyfriend was in his early thirties still living at home with his mother and had abused and neglected her in the same way, blowing her off throughout their entire relationship and regularly cheating on her.

But that wasn't enough for this clown. When she finally mustered the courage to dump him once and for all, he had the sickening gall to prey on her compassionate nature by sending her countless messages begging to get her back. He didn't do it because he genuinely cared about her needs or health, only to control and manipulate her using her bleeding heart to her own detriment.

Laci showed me his messages and they instantly reminded me of a four year old throwing a temper tantrum to get what he wants from parents who haven't established clear rules and consequences. Everything was 'l need, I want, you need to give me' rather than any of it being about her. With my consolation and step by step coaching and translation of his true meaning and intentions, I helped her decode his bullshit.

While she was with him her sleep patterns were horribly disrupted. She woke up at all times during the night in cold sweats, had to wear mouth guards to stop her teeth from being worn away by grinding and she was on anti depressants which weren't even appropriate for her bodies chemistry. This guy did a real number on her and he was ever so close to being next on my short list.

Getting his personal information from her had been exceedingly easy. I would email her questions like 'what's his street address?', 'What's his full name?' and 'What's his email address?' I expected a tiny amount of screening from her like asking me why I wanted to know but all I got was direct answers, almost like she was encouraging me. I doubt the information would have been so readily available if she knew the intimate details of my new hobby.

I don't copy cat the style of Dexter Morgan. I don't have steady access to high power tranquilizers or the free time to stalk someone to get to know their routine well enough. I also don't keep souvenirs or trophies so I don't own a rose-wood box with blood slides or anything quaint like that. My butchering tools are also more hands on rather than going powered since high speed spinning devices tend to make more spatter mess and I'd like to avoid a total blood bath if I can.

Laci sent me an email the next morning apologizing for the hurtful things she said to me when I had called the response units. She regaled me with her tales of how the night went, the psych pro they sent and the adventures of being poked prodded, examined and so forth. I was just glad to hear she still had a pulse. I told her she could repay me for saving her life by never doing that ever again.

Laci has people in her life besides me who love her and depend on her. Even those two runt mutts would lose their spoiled lifestyle with her gone. I just couldn't stand the thought that a pig like Evan would be the reason she took her own life. He was so much lower than scum on the food chain that it would be nothing short of tragic to pay him any kind of compliment by making him think he was that important or had that much impact on anyone's life. And he was messed up enough to take it as a compliment too.

The night had taken a lot out of me so far and I just wasn't up to dumping a body out in the middle of nowhere. I was blasted so I decided to hit the sack and get up early to do it in the morning. It was halfway through fall anyway and it would stay dark until 8:00 am. If I got up at five, I'd have more than enough time to get the job done.

My alarm clock woke me up gently to the soft sounds of the easy rock station. That beeping noise all alarm clocks have drives aggravation and annoyance into my bone marrow when I hear it. Even when they use it in commercials I want to throw a brick at my television and that's just no way to start the day. Maybe Rod Stewart and a couple of DJ's who are mistaken about how funny they are isn't much better but it's a lot easier on the brain pan.

I geared up, got everything I needed to get going including a simple steak knife to cut the bags open quickly and silently moved through the house and out the door. It's moments like that that made me glad I had done little home improvement tasks like spraying WD40 in the hinges to eliminate the creaking. I got into my car and took off. There were two bridges over the same river I knew how to get to off the top of my head that would make suitable locations for the dump.

I got to the freeway bridge at the stroke of five thirty. It was still pitch black with no sun in sight. Right away I knew I couldn't do this from the bridge itself. There wasn't enough shoulder to stop without turning on my hazard lights and that would have attracted a cop car like a moth to a flame. There just wasn't anywhere to hide.

Coming off the bridge though there was a path marked by a sign that showed me a potential boat dock. Although it was a lie with no boat dock visible, it could get me to the water. Upon closer inspection of the area though I realized it just wasn't suitable. The only way to get to the waters edge was by traversing a very steep slope covered in loose rocks and I would have bet money that lugging heavy hefty bags down it would have me slipping to serious injury without fail.

I also wasn't comfortable with the layout under the bridge. It was too dark to tell but there boxes everywhere that I couldn't identify and if I wasn't sure it wasn't a surveillance camera, I didn't want to take the chance. I left the same way I came in and moved on to my next choice.

This one was more rural, further out of town between two farming communities and would have been ideal except that by the time I got there my timing was no longer optimal. The early birds had come out to play and the commuters were getting an early start to beat the morning rush hour traffic. I was pooched, having chosen sleep over peak timing and had to consider waiting yet again to get rid of this thing. I decided to head back to my parents place and recoup.

On the forty five minute drive I tried to search for a solution. I asked myself If burning wouldn't work and bridge drop was out, what other way could I dump these parts in a safe unseen way? Once again necessity is the mother of invention and my need to get rid of this evidence brought the solution to me like a child showing a parent their latest pencil crayon drawing.

The sewer. Of course, how obvious. No one ever goes down there. The body would rot away completely before anyone ever discovered the bones and by then it would be way too late to identify the person.

Once again everything got lighter. I grabbed breakfast at a coffee donut place and ate it in the car on the way to my destination. A banana nut muffin, a double chocolate donut and a café mocha. I love caffeinated beverages but I can't stand the taste of black coffee so as long as it can be dressed up not to taste like coffee, I'm all about it.

I chose the Eastern suburb of the city to dump my waste. It would be practically a ghost town with most of its residents either having commuted to work in the city or otherwise occupied and away from their homes. The housing in this part of my world was also older, done back in the sixties and seventies when neighborhoods were not so congested so there were back alleys to be had. Newer neighborhoods have the homes grouped so close together with attached garages facing the street that alleys don't exist in the new city plans anymore.

Within a few moments I found exactly what I was looking for; a manhole cover placed off to the side behind a power pole. I parked in an empty driveway and popped the trunk. Although it was broad daylight I wasn't worried. No one appeared to be around and I was checking throughout the entire process. Lifting the cover was a piece of cake and my arms gave me no complaint, the pain gone finally. I removed the hefty bags one at a time from the trunk and walked them over the three paces it took to reach the sewer.

With each bag I sliced the tops off and turned them upside down letting the pieces fall into the sewer hearing the splashing sounds as they touched down. I crumpled the bags up, put them back in the trunk and then closed it. I got back in the car, fired her up and took off. My total time there could not have been longer than three minutes max.

I drove back to the kill room to finish destroying evidence. Once there, I packed my trunk remnants into a garbage bag and put everything else in there that needed to burn. Documents from Jims car, receipts, even my empty chip bags. I had five full hefty bags full of garbage that actually would burn, this I knew for a fact. Plastic sheeting, cloth backdrops and paper towels. It may not have been good for the environment but one less person creating pollution for whatever forty some odd more years he would have walked the Earth more than evens that out.

It was funny. This time I burned garbage for a solid three hours making sure nothing was left and did not hear a single siren in a neighborhood where sirens are as common as the sound of a bus stopping and going again. I suppose if my shit hole of an unheated rented detached garage goes up in smoke, no one gives a rats ass, and I was sure there had to be the areas fair share of unemployed people or passersby to call it in if they really wanted to.

To be fair though, plastic burns a lot more colorless than attempted flesh and the smoke was barely visible. The only irritant I had to contend with were the garbage trucks making their rounds up and down the alleys. Every time they would come past I'd have to lid my drum, snuff out my fire, drag it back into the garage and close the door to avoid unwanted attention and then drag it back out and start the process over again.

I used the gas from my jerry can again, soaked all the garbage

———

The available text of Mark Twitchell's "SK Confessions" ends there, mid-sentence.

Online Appendix

Visit my website for additional photos and videos pertaining to the cases in this book:

http://TrueCrimeCaseHistories.com/vol2/

More books by Jason Neal

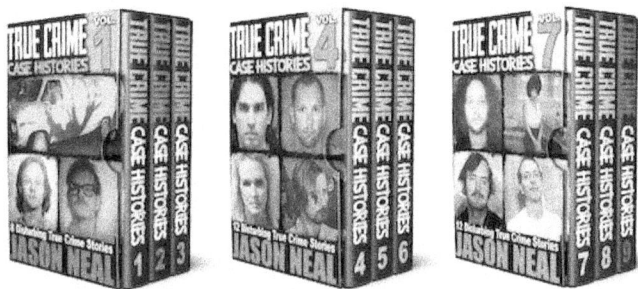

Looking for more?? I am constantly adding new volumes of True Crime Case Histories. The series **can be read in any order,** and all books are also available in paperback, hardcover, and audiobook.

Check out the complete series on Amazon

https://amazon.com/author/jason-neal

or

JasonNealBooks.com

**FREE Bonus Book
For My Readers**

**Click to get
your free copy!**

As my way of saying "Thank you" for downloading, I'm giving away a FREE true crime book I think you'll enjoy.

https://TrueCrimeCaseHistories.com

Just click the link above to let me know where to send your free book!

Choose Your Free True Crime Audiobook

Add Audible Narration and Keep the Story Going!
Plus Get a FREE True Crime Audiobook!

Switch between listening to an audiobook and reading on your Kindle. **Plus choose your first audiobook for FREE!**

https://geni.us/AudibleTrueCrime

THANK YOU!

Thank you for reading this Volume of True Crime Case Histories. I truly hope you enjoyed it. If you did, I would be sincerely grateful if you would take a few minutes to write a review for me on Amazon using the link below.

https://geni.us/TrueCrime2

I'd also like to encourage you to sign-up for my email list for updates, discounts and freebies on future books! I promise I'll make it worth your while with future freebies.

http://truecrimecasehistories.com

And please take a moment and follow me on Amazon.

One last thing. As I mentioned previously, many of the stories in this series were suggested to me by readers like you. I like to feature stories that many true crime fans haven't heard of, so if there's a story that you remember from the past that you haven't seen covered by other true crime sources, please send me any details you can remember and I will do my best to research it. Or if you'd like to contact me for any other reason free to email me at:

jasonnealbooks@gmail.com

https://linktr.ee/JasonNeal

Thanks so much,

Jason Neal

ABOUT THE AUTHOR

Jason Neal is a Best-Selling American True Crime Author living in Hawaii with his Turkish-British wife. Jason started his writing career in the late eighties as a music industry publisher and wrote his first true crime collection in 2019.

As a boy growing up in the eighties just south of Seattle, Jason became interested in true crime stories after hearing the news of the Green River Killer so close to his home. Over the subsequent years he would read everything he could get his hands on about true crime and serial killers.

As he approached 50, Jason began to assemble stories of the crimes that have fascinated him most throughout his life. He's especially obsessed by cases solved by sheer luck, amazing police work, and groundbreaking technology like early DNA cases and more recently reverse genealogy.

g BB a d f

www.ingramcontent.com/pod-product-compliance
Lightning Source LLC
Chambersburg PA
CBHW070033030426
42335CB00017B/2408